LIKE A PALM TREE

Brandy Luna

ACKNOWLEDGEMENTS

To my heroic husband, Stephen Luna,

When I say God gave me you, I mean and know that with every fiber of my being. You, my sweet love, are a sheer gift to my messy life. Insane dreams that I believe come from God flow from my heart and fall out of my mouth, and what do you say? "I believe in you. You can do it baby." That right there is why this book has been accomplished. The days I wanted to give up, the days I didn't know what I was doing, the days of not knowing how I would do it, you always reminded and reassured me that Gods timing for this book, and His plan was perfect. To not worry, and just write. You would affirm me on my insecure days, give me a back massage and tell me, "Remember babe, people's lives will be impacted, so get back to it." I could never express my gratitude for you, my handsome love. Having you as my husband and life partner is God's grace to me. Thank you for believing in me and for leading me to believing in myself so that this book didn't stay a dream but became a reality. I love you baby!

To my God-fearing Mother,

You are the epitome of strength Mom. I'll never forget the first time I truly seen Jesus in someone was in you. Your story inspires me, and I know will continue to inspire others. I'm beyond proud that God chose you to be my Mother. Without you, this book would not exist. You are truly someone who can turn around and say to anyone struggling "I've been redeemed, and you can be too."

I love you Momma. My cheerleader and best friend. I pray this book makes you proud to own your story as God has helped me own mine.

To my Beloved Sisters, Alexis and Jasmine,

You two have endured pain and suffering and have overcome many silent battles. I wrote this book with you both in my heart. I saw your childlike faces in my head, and it would push me to keep going. You two have always unknowingly helped me to keep going. Giving up could never be an option because I always had two little girls that had the same blood in their veins as me that had their eyes on my life. God knew I needed you two. I love ya'll more than I could ever put into words.

DEDICATION

I dedicate this God breathed story to every reader who has ever, or is currently suffering from neglect, sexual, mental, verbal and or physical abuse, homelessness, an eating disorder, and being father or motherless. As well as a special dedication to every foster child who ever lays eyes on this book. You, Beloved, are seen, you are heard, and you are loved by a very real God. Though it may sometimes feel as though you are alone, please trust that you never are. Don't you dare give up! Pray like crazy and keep dreaming! Amazing things are ahead for you. I wish I could hug you!

"The Lord bless you and keep you; the Lord make His face
shine on you and be gracious to you; the Lord
turn His face toward you and give you peace."
Numbers 6:24-26 (New International Version)

CHAPTER

One

"I'm about to do it Aubri, I'm going to run." I whispered, nudging my new cute and petite fourteen-year-old friend, who I had just met the day before.

"I'm going to go to the restroom. When I go, wait for about five minutes. If you see that the staff hasn't noticed that I'm gone, come to the restroom to tell me, okay? Can you do that?" Aubri looked at me with fear and worry in her big brown eyes, but with the smallest shake of her head, she agreed. Getting up out of the chair was my biggest challenge. Fear had my body glued to that old dingy two-dollar movie theater seat, and I was shaking mildly; but I couldn't let the fear take over. This was decided the minute the staff offered a night out for the teens. I had to do it, I had to run away. It was my only chance to get away from the foster care system. Get away from the rules that told me I couldn't see or talk to my family. I was tired of the multitude of caseworkers, counseling sessions, and endless broken promises. The last straw was now being trapped at The Children's Home of Lubbock, away from my sisters because my foster parents couldn't handle me anymore.

"They got me messed up" is the phrase I remember telling myself my first night there at that emergency shelter. I had to do it. I had to run. I couldn't back down now.

Still my hands were shaking uncontrollably with major nerves and anxiety. I gently closed my eyes, took a deep breath, rose to my feet and walked up through the theater aisle and out to the restroom. To my surprise there was no one in there; so, I paced. Up and down that five-stall gray and white narrow restroom for about five minutes that seemed like an everlasting eternity. Desperately hoping that the children's home staff didn't notice me casually leaving the theater room. I hoped they were intrigued with the movie that they picked for us teens to watch. I hoped that they were so distracted by how tasty their buttery popcorn was to where the thought of one of us running wasn't even on their radar. Oh, how I hoped.

Then, to my relief, Aubri finally barged through the restroom door.

"They haven't noticed!" she said, nervously breathing heavily.

"Are you sure?"

"Yes, they're stuck on the movie. If you're gonna go, you should go now. Go Brandy." I could tell by the look in her eyes that she believed in me. Taking another deep breath, I embraced her into my shaking arms, took one last look into those eyes and thanked her. I was so glad to have met her. Such a bold and strong little girl she was. With a heartbreaking story of her own.

"Wait!" she stopped me before walking out. "Here's fifty cents, just in case you find a payphone to call someone. Be careful Brandy, I really hope you make it to wherever you're going." She said sincerely.

We hugged one last time and I walked out of the bathroom with sweaty palms; my jaw quivering but locked in place with a straight and lying face that I had become a pro at giving off. Passing a security guard standing by the door, I innocently smiled at him as I pushed the front theater door open as if I were there on my own, letting him know with my eyes I was just another customer there at the theater, simply leaving. Walking at a normal pace toward a Dairy Queen that was in the same parking lot in front of the theater, my heart nearly pounding out of my small chest, mouth so dry my tongue could stick to the top of my mouth, mind racing a thousand miles an hour expecting to hear "Brandy!" at any second. Yet, as I walked and I walked, no voice. Finally, reaching the Dairy Queen that stood less than a football field distance in front of the theater, I turned a corner taking a few steps to the front of the fast food restaurant where I was no longer in sight of the theater.

I headed for the busy street, looked both ways, waiting for the last car to pass before the next green light. As soon as I saw the last car pass by, I did it. I ran. It was as if my gift of love for running suddenly kicked in and I ran as if I was the last leg in a sixteen- meter run, and the baton was just handed to me. Arms pumping, knees high, controlled breathing, I zoomed through a random suburb neighborhood, passing brick house after brick house, I dared not look back. I feared that if I looked back, I would see the big white van from the children's home behind me, coming to get me and take me back to what I thought was a children's prison. I ran until I spotted an alley ahead.

When I reached that alley, I made my way to the first brown dingy dumpster and collapsed behind it to catch my breath. Gasping for air, mouth still as dry as an Arizona desert, sweat pouring down my tired face from running away in the beating West Texas summer heat, I began to sob. Rivers of tears and cheap Cover Girl mascara running down my sixteen-year-old plump cheeks, my mind was still racing. Sitting there, almost in disbelief that I did it; but also scared of what was to come. Was I going to be able make it in this world without getting caught? If I got caught would they send me so far away that I wouldn't even be able to think about my family like my case investigator told me when I was caught writing my mom in prison? Is this thing called life just some sick joke?

"Ugh!" I remember quietly groaning out loud while looking up with continued sobs.

"My life sucks, I hate this. Why did this have to be my life? I paused in utter frustration and stress. "God, are you even real? Do you even exist!?" I cried hopeless tears, feeling alone. Never did I expect this to be my story. Never did I think I'd be on the run. "Why?" Is all my sixteen-year-old mind could think at that moment. I allowed my breathing to calm down before gathering my emotions, a skill I was used to applying, tucked away all my fears and doubts in my heavily burdened heart, and got up once again to continue running.

CHAPTER

Two

"Get out! Leave Elias! I don't want you here! We don't need you!" I watched my mom as she screamed with tears in her eyes and shoved my intoxicated dad who came in stumbling at a late hour. It broke my four-year-old heart to see her so hurt yet being so aggressive. I could almost feel her anger towards him. The rage in her shaky voice dampened my heart. *Why was she that upset with him? He loved us! Why was she being so mean? And why was she telling him to leave?* I didn't want him to leave. I loved my daddy. He was so great! He always tickled me, told me scary stories, drove fast in the red car to make me giggle, and simply made me feel loved and safe. I loved him, I never wanted him to leave. But for some reason, my mom was persistent on making him walk out of the door he came stumbling in. They argued for a few minutes, although my mom wouldn't give him much chance to speak.

When he could, he would just say "I'm sorry, let's just go to sleep", until my mom physically forced him out of the front door. As he made his swaying way down the front porch, I burst out of my bedroom door where I had been peeking out of and ran after him as he stumbled across our front yard. "Daddy wait! Please don't go! I want you to stay, don't listen to mommy. She's just tired. Please, please, don't go. Can you come back inside and tell me a scary story? Please!" I chased after him across our yard in the dark night.

"Brandy get your butt back over here now!" My mom yelled from the porch.

My dad turned around and kneeled, I could smell beer on his breath, sweat from his pores and fading cologne lingering from his clothes. I knew what beer was from seeing him talk about it and drink it and I knew when he would drink it, he would become different, but none of that ever mattered. He was my daddy and I loved him.

"Mija, you see that big McDonalds sign over there?" he said to me. From where we were standing at mid hours of the dark blue and crisp night, I could see the sign clearly, but it seemed to be far away. "Yes, I see it!" I said.

"Okay" he said, "I'm gonna walk over there and get you a Happy Meal. And then I'm coming right back to tell you a scary story, okay?"

"Oh, okay. Promise daddy? You promise you're coming back?"

"Yes mija, I promise. Now go back inside with your mom before she comes over here and spanks you." He chuckled. "I love you Brandy."

"I love you daddy, so much. I'll be waiting for you, okay?"

"Okay mija. Go inside." As he rose from his knee, he kissed my forehead and walked away into the lonely night, toward the McDonalds sign.

I ran back inside with high hopes, passed my mom; upset with her for being so mean to my dad and went straight to my bed to wait for my daddy and Happy Meal. My mom told me to go to sleep or I would get a spanking. I told her I was waiting for my daddy, and her response shook my little soul.

"Your dad doesn't love you! He doesn't care about you and he's not coming back; go to sleep!". Even though that hurt to hear, I didn't believe her. I knew my daddy loved me, and she couldn't convince me otherwise. So, I pretended to go to sleep by closing my eyes and pulling my pink flowered blanket over my curly brown hair, and I waited; and waited and waited until my eyelids eventually covered my dark brown eyes for the night.

The next morning, I woke up abruptly and looked around, remembering what had happened before falling asleep. I quickly got up from my bed and went straight for my mom and dad's room, fully expecting for my dad to be there; but, to my huge surprise, no daddy. I went to the bathroom, nothing. The kitchen, nothing. I even snuck outside through the side kitchen door while my mom was still sleeping and checked the side shed where my daddy and my Tio would sometimes drink beer, nothing. My heart sank and tears glazed over my eyes. *"Maybe he'll be here later"* I thought.

Except that day passed by without my daddy showing up, and days after that as well. Those days soon turned into weeks, then into months, and yet, still no daddy. At this point, the echo of my Mom's voice, and the first lie that the enemy filled my little four-year-old heart with *your dad doesn't love you, he doesn't care about you, and he's not coming back.* Those thoughts would play in my head almost daily. I missed my dad, I still loved him, and wanted him to come back more than anything.

As time passed; true pain began to make itself at home in my little heart. I began to wonder what I did wrong for my daddy to leave me. *Why didn't he like me anymore? What did I do to make him mad at me?* I would think about how I should have picked up my stuffed animals the first time he told me to, or to eat all my food when he asked instead of telling him I wasn't hungry anymore. I would just think and think about everything I should have done better for him, so he wouldn't have left. It was all my fault, I just knew it. I thought my mom pushed him away that night, but it was me. I pushed him away. As time passed with those questions and hurt hidden in my heart, it came to be just me and mom. We moved a lot and stayed at a lot of different places. I didn't mind though. I had to make sure that I did everything right and not misbehave so my mom wouldn't leave me too.

We ended up living with my grandma for a little while. As a five going on six-year-old, that was fun. My aunt, who was the youngest sister of my mom's siblings, would always show me the coolest songs by Snoop Dog, Destiny's Child, Master P and all the other hip artists that were dropping hip hop, rap and R&B hits in the 90's. My Uncle who was the youngest of all my mom's siblings, would always want me to play his Nintendo 64 with him when he didn't have friends to play with. Life wasn't so bad in my mind.

Until one day, something strange happened. It was a cloudy day outside and everyone was gone except my mom who was napping. I wanted to go outside so bad to play, but I knew my mom was going to say no if I asked her. I decided to do what I always did if mom was asleep: sneak out. I quietly cracked open the back door that was in my Tia's room and slipped out as slowly and as sneaky as possible. Once I made it out without my mom waking up, I made my way next door where my cousin Jared who was around my age lived to see if he was outside to play. As I approached his porch, the clouds began to sprinkle. I contemplated turning back to go home but an older kid (by maybe ten years older or so) that I'd recognized from the neighborhood had occupied an orange chair on my cousin's porch, and yelled out to me.

"Hey! Jared's not home but you can come over here and wait for him with me so you're not in the rain." He almost insisted. I hesitated, but for some reason couldn't say no and go home the way I felt I should. I walked up to my cousin's white house with black trimming and stepped onto the humble porch.

"Here, you can sit down right here." Patting an identical orange chair next to his. I sat.

"Do you like rain?" he asked, trying to strike up a conversation.

"I don't know," I said hesitantly.

"You don't know?" he paused, "Well, do you like this?"

Leaning over my five-year-old body, he clasped the two sides to my chair and pulled it to where the front of each chair were almost touching, if it weren't for my little legs in the middle. He then placed his hands on my legs and spread them open to where they were dangling on the outsides of the chair and pulled my chair closer to where the front of the chairs then touched. He then picked up my legs and pulled them around him. I was frozen. I didn't know what to think or feel. Forcefully, he pulled my body towards him to where both our bodies were in full contact, and no part of me felt that it was right. Frightened, words began to spill out of my mouth.

"No, stop it." I began to push away. Thankfully he let go and pushed me away aggressively.

"Fine you big baby. Get out of here then!" he said as he shoved my chair away. Quickly, I hopped off the chair, ran to my grandmas and made my way quietly through her back door. My mom was still sleeping. Part of me wanted to wake her up and tell her what happened, but more of me knew I would get a spanking for going outside and probably get in trouble for the incident anyway. Because it just felt so wrong, I knew I couldn't tell anyone. It was all my fault. I shouldn't have gone outside, I thought. Now as an adult, I can't help but think about what caused that kid to act on me that way. What was done to him?

Kindergarten is the grade I was in at this time and all I can remember is having the urge to take things that weren't mine. It made me feel like I had control of something if I simply took things I wanted when no one was watching.

Nap time came around one day and as a reward for being asleep, my teacher would tip toe around and drop a lollipop on our nap towel so we would wake up to it. I pretended to be asleep and saw a root beer

lollipop gently land next to my head. I wasn't a fan of root beer and noticed that my classmate who was legitimately asleep next to me got a raspberry one. My favorite. I waited for my moment, and quickly snatched his raspberry lollipop and tucked it under my towel without replacing it with my root beer one.

When it was time to wake up, my classmate was confused about him not having a lollipop. My teacher must have seen guilt all over me because she immediately asked me to unroll my towel and sure enough, two lollipops rolled out onto the floor. She had a talk with me but that didn't keep me from doing it again. As a five-year-old, I began to love the thrill and satisfaction of taking what wasn't mine. Finally resulting in being sent to the principal's office for having another classmate's huge cute bow tucked in my shirt during play time, and for being the suspect of my teachers missing bell from her desk, my mom was called in for a meeting.

When my mom never showed up, I was relieved and dared not show her the note that was sent home with me. My backpack wasn't being checked at home anymore anyway. Ever since leaving our own house and moving in with my grandma. My mom's behavior was slowly changing before my eyes regarding little things like kissing my head before school and such. The little things that meant the world to me. Speaking of, she and I didn't last long at my grandma's that time around.

After maybe a few months, I remember being awake late at night watching Barney in my grandma's living room while my mom was in the bathroom. I remember how I always tried my best to stay up to make sure she didn't leave me. My mom was always in the bathroom now. Sometimes alone, or sometimes with a friend. She would be in there for a long time then come out with her mouth moving in a weird way and gently but constantly pulling on her hair under her ears with her pointer finger and thumb. She would always be so quiet while picking at her hair, with her face a little sweaty, and would just peak out of the window as if she was waiting for someone or scared that someone might show up. I learned to get used to this behavior. If she didn't leave me like my dad did, I didn't care what she did…I loved her. So yes, that late night of me watching Barney. My mom was in the bath-room, when my grandma swung open the front door and came stumbling in.

"Where's your mom?" She asked while breathing heav-ily. I knew she had been drinking. I just gave her a blank stare not knowing what to say or what was about to hap-pen. She made her way through the living room, and to the restroom where my mom was.

I heard the bathroom door swing open. "Get out!! Find somewhere else to stay!

And get that stuff out of here!" She slurred and yelled in pain from whatever she saw. I heard repetitive slaps against my mom and commotion. I began to tear up and mentally freak out. I didn't know what was about to hap-pen.

My mom came out and around the corner of the living room crying, grabbed me and her car keys, shoved the front door open, hurried down my grandma's narrow front porch steps, put me in the passenger seat, started the car, and we drove off headed down the dirt hill in the middle of the night. Crying and scared, I asked "mommy where are we going?".

"I don't know Brandy, I don't know!" She yelled and cried as well, zooming down a dirt hill. Then, after what it seemed like forever being trapped in the car from stopping at a strange house and having to wait in the car after leaving my grandmas, we pulled up to a familiar house.

My Welas house. She was my grandma's mom. She always had the best sweet bread on her table and cable where I could watch the good cartoons. I was relieved to pull up to a familiar and safe place. We got off and I remember my mom tapping on my Welas window.

"Wela, it's Mima", my mom voiced as she gently tapped.

Finally, my Wela answered the door. Without a word, she opened the door to me and my mom and walked back to her bedroom.

"Lay there on the couch and go to sleep." My mom told me. As she made her way through my Welas kitchen and to her restroom where she stayed for the rest of the night.

CHAPTER

Three

Many seasons had passed, I was coming on seven years old that year and my mom and I were back at Grandmas. Only this time, my Grandma had lived in a new house. A faded yellow, two-bedroom trailer with chipped brown trimming that was one block away from the softball park there on the west side of Brownfield. I liked living there because my friends that I met at school lived right around the corner. My mom would sometimes let me walk over and play with them when she had to go somewhere and would *be right back*. I had just begun second grade at the *big girl* school, Oakgrove Elementary.

I can remember being so excited to ride the yellow bus that I could hardly contain myself. The first ride to school was scary but also so liberating. There I was all by myself at the corner of my grandma's yard where my mom had told me to stand and wait. I indeed felt like such a big girl. There it came, the big girl bus. It stopped and with a loud wham, the bus doors swung open. I took a deep breath, curly hair in a high ponytail, wearing my one and only pink Rugrats overalls, with my glittery pink jelly shoes sparkling. I was sure to own this day on the bus, and second grade. Step by step, I went up.

"Morning, pick any seat." The bus driver said with no enthusiasm. I smiled as best as I could at him. He halfway smiled back. I turned to my left to see so many rows of olive-green seats to my left and right. *Where to sit?* I walked and walked then saw an empty seat towards the back and to the right and sat down. The ride was smooth and quiet from where I was sitting, and I indeed enjoyed the ride, over hearing other kids talk about their new school clothes and school supplies. Stop after stop and I would hear, "Morning! Pick any seat.".

After a while, the bus finally pulled into the school parkway and off we went to our school day. Everything was so fun! The learning and playing with other kids. Which is where I was able to meet my friends from my neighborhood. Then, once the school day was over, it was time to hop on the bus and head home to tell my mom and grandma all about what I had done during my first day of second grade. That's

when I realized that my school friends rode the same bus as me! Which is also how I found out where they lived. In fact, as a bonus, my grandma knew both of their moms. Going over to their houses always made me feel comfortable. There were many similarities between our lifestyle and theirs. It was what I began to see life was.

Second grade continued to be great, other than when my bus rides home became miserable with a girl who bullied me. She would intentionally sit behind me and pull my hair and say things to try and make me cry like I looked ugly, or how I was poor because of how my house looked. But besides her, it was fine from what I remember. However, home life was getting a little more complicated. My mom started disappearing more and more, and when she was home, I hardly remember ever spending time with her. She was always on the move with this new boyfriend she had. I remember meeting him very briefly before my mom went off with him for yet another (what it seemed like to a six-year-old) long time.

I was often confused though, because she also had another guy friend that would come around quite often. We even went on a trip to Houston with him at a certain time. He would just pop in at random and then I wouldn't see him for a good while. I never understood that situation; but again, he was nice. One time he gave me a dollar, and I was so excited about it until I lost it.

I never even realized I lost it until my mom asked me for it and I couldn't find it.

"FIND IT!" She screamed. Scrambling through piles and piles of dirty clothes that were on the floor in the room she and I slept in. I never found it, and I was spanked for it. I remember becoming scared of my mom over time. She began to progressively become someone completely different and I couldn't understand why. She no longer cooked for me, watched movies with me, or even really asked me questions about anything anymore. Nothing of what she used to do. I loved my mom so much, but I started to feel like she didn't love me anymore. Especially when I began to see her stomach get bigger and finding out that I was going to be a big sister. Which I was not excited about whatsoever. What could I do or say to change it? I didn't want a sister or a brother. I just wanted my mom to stay home with me and love me like she used to, but it just wasn't happening. Another day came again where she left me with a family friend while she and my aunt went to *the store*. It was as if the second they drove off, the guy wasted no time, popped a VHS tape in the VCR and told me we were going to watch something. "I want to watch The Lion King", I remember telling him.

"We'll watch that after we watch this okay?" he told me. It was then on this video he was forcing me to watch where I saw things that I had never seen before. The tape contained grownups doing very inappropriate things that made me feel so uncomfortable. At a point, I remember squeezing my eyes closed wishing he would turn it off, but he wouldn't.

"Watch it. If you're a big girl like you say you are, you'll open your eyes and watch it." He coaxed me. Being a big girl meant the world to me for some reason. There was something about being called a big girl that made me feel a sense of strength; so, I watched. As I sat there, internally disgusted, because no one had to tell me what we were watching was wrong. I felt it in my six-year-old gut. After about fifteen minutes of watching the disgusting movie, the guy stood up.

"Come here", he said as he grabbed my hand, pulled me up and led me into the bedroom. My little body froze to ice cold. Images from the movie we had just watched flashed in my head and I was terrified. Tears filled my eyes in terror. My God given innocents were taken from me. I felt empty, confused and petrified at the same time. I didn't know how to put it together in my head of what was happening. Or why. I just wanted to escape mentally.

Later on, when it was all said and done, my mom and aunt came back for me. Nothing was said about anything that happened. I felt ashamed and guilty. How could I even describe what happened if I ever gained the courage to say something. I didn't know what happened! I just knew it was so very wrong and a little part of me, Brandy, went missing. The voice inside of my head told me that I for sure would have got in trouble if I said a word. There was my very first dark secret that I dared not let anyone know.

CHAPTER

Four

The year was 1999, one year after my first sister, Alexis was born. I was then around eight. We had moved from living with my grandma to living with one of my mom's friends. Her friend had three boys around my age, and my mom had Alexis and me. Our time there was for a short season, but I remember quite well that we all stayed in a one-bedroom house off Tahoka Highway there in Brownfield. The house was close to an intermediate school that used to exist, where me and the three boys would walk over to play on the school playground after school hours. I liked living there. It felt as if we were one big family. I didn't mind one bit.

It was another ordinary day of walking over to the school playground to swing, play tag, slide and race. When the sun began to set swiftly, the boys ran home without me, due to me having to put my shoes back on and tie my laces. They teased and laughed as they ran off about me having to walk home alone if I didn't hurry. I cried in frustration trying to tie my complicated shoelaces. By the time I finally got them to where they wouldn't come untied, they were gone. Off I began my short journey home, alone. I thought by taking a short cut, I could get home sooner before dark. The shortcut was through a senior citizen's apartment complex or *where the old people live* is what I used to call it. While walking through that parking lot of the complex, I heard a voice calling me.

"Hey, sh sh, tu!" it called. I looked over to my right where the voice carried from and there sat an older man with a black wife beater, dark blue loose jeans, cowboy boots and wore a brown cowboy looking hat. He was sitting on his apartment porch rocking in an old rustic metal rocking chair.

"Come here!" He said with a smile on his face. Mind you, I was never really taught to not talk to strangers, so me being a naive eight-year-old, I walked over to see what the gentlemen wanted.

"You want a toy mija?" He asked with a struggling English accent.

"A toy? What kind of toy?" I said.

"Come in, I show you." He gestured to me. Scared to say no and run, the way my little gut told me to do, I followed the man inside of his apartment.

"Sit down here and I'll go get it." He said as he turned away from me. I sat down on his twin size bed that he had as his living room sitting arrangement and looked around at the tiny space as he disappeared into a little hallway to the left of the room. The stench smelled old and his walls were a light pink/peachy color, with barely anything hanging on them, giving an empty and lonely feeling. And about four feet in front of the twin size bed that had a rough blue wool blanket spread across was a small metal cart looking table that carried his small boxed TV, with an antenna sticking up on top.

I remember feeling so frightened and looking at his front door thinking *run Brandy*. But I just couldn't, my bottom felt like it was stuck to that springy twin bed. Heart pounding with a knot beginning to develop in my throat, regretting that I went in, he finally came out of whatever room he was in down that hallway. He was carrying a white plastic board that had The Looney Tunes as small plastic characters golfing on top of it. He sat next to me on that bed. He smiled at me and handed me the toy.

"Thank you," I replied, slowly making myself get up. As I rose, he placed his hand on my right shoulder and gave a forceful gesture to sit back down. "I need to go home; my mom will be worried." I said. Knowing my mom probably didn't care where I was. Like a disgusting vampire, he went for my neck and began kissing it. His right hand went to places that made me cry by the uncomfortable motion and absolute violation. His breath smelled awful, his rough mustache was rubbing all over my neck and lips, and I just needed to get up and leave but I couldn't! Once again, I was frozen in fear, nearly blacking out where I sat. My small hands were pushing against his thick chest,

"Please, I need to go home!" I began to cry out loud. Thankfully he stopped. I quickly rose again and headed for the door, tears streaming down my face and heart still pounding. He followed behind and opened the door for me.

"You don't tell no one, tiendes?" (Which is Spanish for "understand?")

"Yes" I said, as I pushed the door open and ran home.

After what it seemed like a short journey made long, I made it home. Not knowing what I was going to say when I walked through the back door, which was the kitchen door.

"Why are you later than the boys?" My mom asked.

"They left me." I sent a glare their way, and in the moment hated and blamed them for what had just happened. I sat the toy on the table, and with no one even asking about it, I headed to the living room to just sit and try to forget what had taken place about fifteen minutes ago. Another tucked away hurt.

Time went on and things seemed to get serious with my mom and her boyfriend, my sister Alexis's dad. So much so, that they decided it was best that we move to another town all together where some of his family lived. Denver City, Texas. A smaller Texas town then the previous one we lived in.

I was almost finished with third grade at my new school, Kelly Dawson Elementary. New school, new faces, new everything really. Which wasn't so bad, other than my mom and now stepdad leaving me with Alexis often while they went *to the store* every other hour. And when they were home, they'd be in the restroom for what felt like hours. I would worry about Alexis while I was at school, hoping they weren't leaving her home alone.

It was hard to focus on learning anything because things in my life had just become so confusing. Thank God school was almost out for summer break. A small moment of clarity in this confusion was that it always felt right when they would take us to church. My stepdad's sister had given her life to Jesus Christ maybe two years or so prior and was influencing both my mom and stepdad to attend. So, there we were, every other Sunday when we could all wake up and be ready on time, we would attend a little ol' Spanish church. I would go to the children's classes and hear about this Jesus man and would love the thought of feeling safe "in His hands" as they'd say. Church was the one place I felt comfort and safety. Not to mention the food that was always served after every Sunday service was always nice.

By living in Denver City, I was able to become close to a friend in the neighborhood who was only a few years older than me. It was always a great time to be able to stay over, sing Ashanti and Jennifer Lopez songs all night, eat junk food and such. I also have distinct memories of taking part in inappropriate behavior with her. Behavior that I knew was wrong in my gut, but out of both she and I being exploited by sexual abuse at such a young age, we became victims to sexual bondage, even with each other by age nine and eleven. However, those sleepovers came to an end when my stepdad made the announcement of us having to move yet again about a month into summer.

"Where are we going now?", I asked him. His answer was a town called Seagraves. It's smaller than Denver City, but he thought we would like it. Off we went, and there we were, another town, another home. And it wasn't long before I realized there would be another sibling as well. It was as if my mom's belly grew overnight once moving there.

I would often pretend I knew my dad's address, and even though I knew he had new daughters from what I was told, I would try to imagine him still loving me and wanting me. I'd write letters to him saying that I hated living with my mom. Asking if he would please come back and get me. Of course, I didn't know how to send letters. All I knew was that he lived in Lubbock. So,

I'd stash them in a drawer where I kept all my little trinkets I'd find around, in hopes that someday I could get them to him somehow. I would sometimes imagine running away in the middle of the night while my mom and stepdad were in the bathroom and walking to Lubbock to find him at a store. Oh, how my imagination would go places.

To my surprise, my stepdad found the letters one day and was noticeably hurt at the intention of me wanting my real dad, I sensed it in his behavior toward me for a little while. It was simply a heavy summer.

Thankfully, it wasn't long before that season was over, school was back in session, and I was the new third grader. Then only a couple of weeks into the season, September of the year 2000 brought us a new sibling. It was a girl, and my mom and stepdad decided to name her Jasmine. I don't really know or remember where this came into play, but Jasmine had a different dad as well. Though my mom and stepdad were still together. It was confusing to me how that came about, but I didn't care. All I know is that we were blessed with a beautiful baby girl. There was always something so sweet about her.

I grew to love both my sisters in such a profound way. Just as I began to adjust to the new school and friends, Christmas break hit that year, and low and behold I was told that we were moving back to Denver City. Not even caring anymore, I'd shrug my

shoulders and would have no choice but to make the best of every move.

Then after that move, and finishing the school year in Denver City, we moved to Andrews, Texas where my aunt Cynthia and Uncle Lonnie lived. I believe we only lived there for a couple of months, about the summertime; out in the country in a trailer before we moved back to Denver City once again. I couldn't take school seriously anymore because I never knew when I would be pulled to a new one.

One thing I could take seriously though was reading. Reading took off the edge for my tiny soul. I was always able to escape the ordinary and get lost in a fictional story. I loved it and excelled in reading to reach the high goals within A.R points. Points that were given each time I finished a book. Yet, in every other subject, I was failing terribly. Which led me to failing that year there at Kelly Dawson Elementary, and having to repeat the grade. I was always just so frustrated and confused in class to the point where I would just give up.

I remember my teacher calling my mom in for a parent teacher conference where she broke the news that I was failing. When we got home, I got beat and told I was going to be the oldest one in my grade the next year. I was sad at the thought, but soon got over it, and moved on mentally.

CHAPTER

Five

Fast forwarding a bit in my life, fifth grade for myself, Kindergarten for Alexis, and Jasmine about two years old. Life would be off and on as far as good went. Some days there would be breakfast made, laughter in the atmosphere with my stepdad always cracking jokes, and no arguing; just talking. Days where I had hope that things were going to change for the better. Where we all five had actual family bonding. Like Christmas time where my mom would receive help from churches to have nice gifts for us under the tree or we'd stay up late together watching movies. Then other days just seemed like it would get worse than before the good days.

Not only at home, but I began to really hate school. I would go to school with clothes that were stained, didn't smell very pleasant, and the popular girls made sure everyone was aware of my stench each time our teacher would leave the classroom for whatever reason.

"Something smells and it's coming from over there." Pointing in my direction. My cheeks would blush, kids would giggle, and I just wanted to scream.

"Ew, look at her old faded clothes." One of the girls would whisper to another as they passed me.

Whatever, I would think. Deep down only dreaming of having cool clothes like them. Not all the girls were mean, I thankfully had friends who saw past the dirty clothes and the extra weight, but those few mean girls never made things easier. I tend to think back and wonder what must have been going on in their homes for them to feel it was okay to bring others down.

Anyhow, back at home, I don't recall what exactly happened, but my stepdad was no longer present. My guess is that my mom and him could never come to an agreement about their work situations. I do recall him having an illness, which resulted in him not being eligible for a decent job. On a normal day, he would be home with us while my mom would work one, sometimes two jobs at McDonalds and or a convenience store called Allsups to pay the light bill and support their habit. Thank God for food stamps and HUD, otherwise, it was McChickens and fried

Allsups burritos every day until food stamps came in. I didn't mind it to much, but it was always nice to have a change in meals.

I believe, over time, my mom became tired of being the financial support system, and all I remember was that my stepdad was no longer a part of our lives from one day to the next. I missed him at times. He was the closest thing I had to a dad since my biological dad left. Despite the bondage him and my mom battled, he was such a funny and caring man. Always tried his best to make things lighter around the house with his humor and cleanliness. Nonetheless, I had to learn to not allow the absence of a father figure get the best of me. Though, deep down, I yearned for it.

There we were, us three girls and my mom in a cute two-story government paid house on the outside, but what had become gloomy and unsafe on the inside. My mom being the kindhearted and decorative woman God created her to be, she would always try and make our houses look pretty with cheap decor. I always appreciated that about her. However, the drug habits had gotten so bad that the house began coming to a crumble before our eyes. House parties were thrown often. Different men in and out of the house. Rap music was always blaring, cussing, arguing, and frustration nearly always flowing, and the house constantly smelling like spray paint from the switch of her and her friends using crack to then huffing spray paint out of socks.

I always did my best to stay close to my sisters. Keeping them upstairs with me while parties were going on. Playing country music as filthy rap would be blaring downstairs. Alexis would cry wanting to be in that scene, but I understood that as a four-year-old, she wouldn't be safe. I would sometimes find myself yelling at her trying to get her to listen to me, to protect her. I even began to take my anger out on her with yelling, then would feel terrible because I hated when my mom would yell at me and knew the feeling. I just didn't know how to release the anger that I had in my soul.

I hated who my mom became. On my worst days, I would reminisce on the days when she was sober, and sound minded as a little girl. She was so loving, caring and kind. Then drugs came in the picture at some point after my dad left and ruined our whole life. I would always wonder why she chose to begin using them from the get-go. Why did she need drugs to make her feel good? I would sometimes beg my mom to stop doing them. Long nights of sitting outside the bathroom door as I knew what she was doing in there. Crying my eyes out, knowing that as she continued to pursue this life, our lives would get worse.

My only escape was when I was able to slip away from my house to my friends' houses. Either Summer or Taylors. At either house I always felt safe. Every chance I got to where I knew my sisters were also safe for the day, I would be at their houses. Homes where normal childhoods were being lived out for the most part. Places where there were good vibes, cleanliness, meals shared together, joking around and normal sibling disagreements. For those short times that I was able to be a part of those scenes were bliss to my soul. No spray paint, no cussing, no unimaginable yelling, no parties, etc. Just family. Yet, when I would head home, it felt like returning to a nightmare. But my sisters would keep my head up. They needed me, and I needed them to keep going.

When parties weren't going on at our house, it seemed as if my mom was either asleep, or gone. What first turned into a few hours of her leaving me to watch the girls had turned into days at a time. There would be some days of missing school due to no one being able to watch Jasmine while Alexis and I went to school. If we were lucky, my grandma who moved to Denver City to be close to us would watch us.

My teacher that year, Mrs. Williams, suspected unsettling things about me by the way she would pay extra attention to me in class. She was always so concerned for my eyesight, having me sit at the very front so I could see what she was teaching on the overhead projector.

She would pull me aside sometimes and simply say "Sweetheart, if you ever feel in your little heart that you need to tell me anything, just know you can, okay?". I loved Mrs. Williams. She had this gracious way of making me feel seen and understood without judgement. So much so that I trusted going with her during lunch to an eye doctor to get glasses that she paid for. My only instruction from her was that I left them at school so that I was sure not to lose them. She was so sweet. I thank God for her and for a few others in my life that I now see were sent by God to love on me, whether they know it or not.

My two friends, Summer and Taylor, are such people that He sent to me. I had grown extremely close to them. Both of their families always treated me as one of their own. Always inviting me over for dinner, to stay the night with their daughter, giving me clothes and other supplies. One thing I noticed as a fourth and fifth grader is that they were never allowed at my house. Maybe once or twice did they come over to play for an hour or so after school. But never could they stay the night. Again, I sure was always grateful for the times I was able to go over or stay at theirs.

People noticed the odd behavior coming from our household; but it took one night to really grab the attention that we as children and as a single mother who was so lost needed. It was dead winter during Christmas break there in Denver City. Our home had no electricity, no heat, just running water. My mom was gone, and Alexis's cough was keeping all three of us up. Along with her cough, my right ear was pounding with an ache that was excruciating. I could do nothing but bundle us up the best I could with our jackets on and blankets piled on us. Until Alexis began to vomit from her cough worsening. At that point I felt helpless. My heart hurt so much for her. I looked over to my other sister Jasmine with boogers running down her sweet innocent face, not being able to breathe through her nose, and I just began to sob. I had to think of something to help Alexis. I felt as if I had no choice but to bathe her in freezing cold water to wash the vomit out of her hair as quickly as I could then get her wrapped back in blankets. Once that was accomplished, I was fed up with that night. I needed my mom home.

Even though she was mostly useless when she was home by sleeping or getting high, I just needed someone older than me to be present so that I didn't feel as helpless and alone. *Think Brand*, I thought. I curiously looked out of the front living room window to see if maybe a neighbor's light would be on, even though I had no clue as to what time it was. Thankfully, the neighbors living room light from across the street was on. It was the moment

I decided to make a move. I bundled up as best I could, told Alexis to watch over Jasmine while I went to use the phone to call our mom, and headed for the neighbor's house.

Light drizzly ice fell from the dark blue sky as I walked across the lonely street at only God knows what time of night. With nerves running a little wild, knowing how upset my mom would be once she received this phone call I was about to make, I stood

at the doorstep of that neighbors for a brief second, took a deep breath and knocked.

Then knocked again, and once more before leaving. Then suddenly I hear the front door unlock and see a face. A kind yet concerned woman's face. She had short, choppy brunette hair.

Wrapped in a white robe she responded, "can I help you mija?".

"Yes, my mom went to see my grandma. Can I use your phone to call her?" I have no idea where that lie came from, but that's all I was taught to do when being questioned by anyone. Otherwise, mom would be upset.

"Of course, come in.", she gestured me into her home. Still carrying the concerned look on her face, I walked into her warm, welcoming and cozy home. Just standing there could put me to sleep if I let it.

"The phones over here mija." She led me to her kitchen where a house phone was connected. "Do you want some hot chocolate?".

"No thank you." I said, despite deep down wanting some more than I could say. Having my freezing cold sisters across the street, I wouldn't dare take that blessing without them. I stood with the house phone in my hands desperately trying to remember the phone number to the phone that my mom had just got from a man that would give her money from time to time. I could feel the lady about three feet away from me in her kitchen waiting to hear my conversation with my mom. I looked back with a shy look that said *can I please have a minute?* She read the words in my head and walked away. Click! The number appeared in my tired mind and I dialed.

"Hello." My mom answered with a soft-spoken voice and no noise in the background.

At that moment, I already knew she was high. Each time she was home and in the bathroom for what it seemed to be hours; she was as quiet as a mouse. She would come out every now and then to peak the window. Sweaty, shiny face. Pulling on her hair at the bottom of her scalp. Then go back to the bathroom.

"Mom, it's Brand. Alexis is really sick, and I have a really bad earache and I'm scared mom. Will you please come home?" I begged quietly into the phone.

"Where are you calling me from, little girl?!" She said in a panic.

"The neighbors. Their light was on and I needed to get a hold of you." I replied.

"Go back home right now little girl. I'll be there in a minute!"

"Promise mom?" With tears beginning to glaze over my helpless eyes.

"GO HOME BRANDY." Click. I hung up the neighbor's phone with my head hanging. Knowing I couldn't take her word of coming home soon.

"Do you want to bring your sisters over here until your mom gets home mija?" My sweet neighbor asked.

"No, we're okay. My mom said she's on her way. She should be home any minute." With my insides screaming yes.

"Okay, well, just come over if she takes too long okay. I'll be up", she said walking me to the front door.

I left her home and walked back to mine wishing I could have stayed. Wishing I could have told the truth of what was going on. I made it back home safely, sisters sound asleep cuddled together, on the living room couch where I left them. Wiggling my body in the blankets with theirs, breathing in cold air, I finally fell asleep.

'KNOCK, KNOCK, KNOCK.' My eyes shot wide open; relief ran through my body thinking it was my mom knocking to let her in. Not checking who it was, I unlocked and opened the front door, and a bright light shined through my little pupils.

"Hi there. How are you tonight sweetheart?" My heart thumped and began beating obnoxiously, and my stomach sank down my shivering legs. I froze in fear. It was a cop.

What did I just do? My mom is gonna kill me, I thought.

"Sweetie?" said the cop. I snapped out of it and had to think fast. "Fine, officer."

"Well good, can I ask what your name is?" he asked. "Brandy".

"Okay Brandy, do you think I could speak with your mom or dad?" he quietly asked. Mind scrambling on what lie to tell, I quickly remembered the lie that I told the neighbor.

"My mom went to go see my grandma in Brownfield. My grandma got really sick and put in the hospital and my mom needed to be there with her." Straight face showing no fear or sign of a fib; but feeling like I could fall over at any moment inside.

"Well alright then." Shining his flashlight inside our living room. "Are those your siblings?" The light beamed on my sick sisters cuddled together on the couch. "Yes sir".

He continued to shine his light all over the living room while still standing at the front door. I remember him staring at the Dorito bag on the coffee table and I felt relieved thinking he wouldn't think our situation was so bad because it appeared like we had food.

"Alright then, Miss Brandy. Can I ask you to do something important for me?" The police officer reached for his wallet and pulled out a card. "Can you have your mom give me a call when she gets home? My name and number is on this card. Just be sure to give this to her, okay?" He said with a kind, caring tone of voice.

"Yes sir, I can do that".

"Well alright then. You keep this door locked and I look forward to hearing from your mom here soon alright?", he replied.

"Yes sir", I replied while already deciding I wasn't going to tell her. First of all, God only knew when she would be home, and secondly, I would be beat had she known a cop came looking for her due to me using the phone across the street. I knew it was the neighbor who called. I somewhat felt mad, yet glad that she did.

CHAPTER

Six

Oh yes, summertime yet again. That dreadful winter had come and gone, as well as spring, then this sweet season showed her sun shining face. Also, the time of year where I was able to get away for a few weeks and spend time with my favorite cousin there in Brownfield. Amber is the same age as me and throughout the younger years, when my mom left me here or there for her outings, Amber's house was one of those places I was left at. It also happened to be my favorite place to stay. She always had all the cool toys, a trampoline, swimming pool, and the best Disney movies on VHS. I remember putting our imaginations together to make our own songs and plays, then performing them for our imaginary crowd. Putting on a garage sale to sell her old toys to earn money to go to thecity swimming pool, and not having one single customer. Still feeling accomplished that we organized and actually had our own garage sale. Being at her house was always a dream for me. It was a place where I was free to be a kid. Though her mom and dad were always on the move, us two were always given the perfect things to keep us occupied.

One hot summer day, we begged her mom over the phone to allow us to go to the swimming pool and our begging worked in just the right way. After picking up Amber's room, her mom finally caved and had my aunt, Amber's grandma, drive us to take a dip at the city pool. What a blast it was. Seeing kids your age left and right. Remembering a few faces from when I use to go to school there a few years back. Getting in line to jump off the diving boards, doing tricks in the pool. Just a nice refreshing and fun time. Until an idyllic moment in time was stopped with just one sentence. I was sitting on the side of the pool more towards the deep end of the rectangular shaped pool. My feet were dangling in the water, the sun shining on my dry face, as I watched other kids jumping off of the diving board, showing off with their jumping tricks, with not a care in the world.

"Brandy!" I heard. The voice didn't sound too familiar, then I turned around towards the voice that was trying to get my attention.

"Brandy! Come here mija!" My sister Alexis's aunt called me from the outside part of the fence around the pool. I quickly rose and walked over to her in full curiosity as to why in the world she was calling me so randomly.

"Mija, do you know where your sisters are!?" she asked me.

"Uhm, with my mom in Denver City, why?" I replied in a curious tone.

"No mija, your sisters were taken away by CPS (Child Protective Services). You need to come with me. Hurry grab your things and meet me out here at my car", she told me in a hushed voice.

Her sentence right there. Those words that my sisters, my two helpless, probably scared to death sisters had been put in the care of the state dropped my heart down to my feet and sent my little body into an angry yet fearful shiver. I quickly grabbed my shoes, ran over to Amber where she was laying out getting some sun and told her we had to go. She was confused but just followed considering my serious and terrified facial expression. We both got in Alexis's Aunt's 2002 emerald green Chevy Malibu and she drove off.

"Where are we going? Where are my sisters?" I asked with hot tears already filling my eyes.

"I'm taking you to Onkas (Ambers house)." She replied in a clipped voice. When I sensed that that's all she could say, I just sat in silence, mind running rampant and heart pounding. Amber just sat on the opposite side of the back seat with worry in her eyes as well. About five minutes later we pulled up to Amber's house just an hour after leaving the pool. I ran inside looking for someone, anyone with answers. And there sat Veronica, Amber's mom with a phone in her hands. She looked at me with eyes that screamed *I'm sorry*. I grabbed the phone to see who was on the other line, hoping I'd finally get some answers.

"Brand, it's Cynth." My aunts (my mom's middle sister) familiar voice vibrated through the phone.

"Cynthia! Where's my sisters?! Where's my mom?! What's going on?!" Tears streamed down my face, frightened with no answers.

"Your mom is stupid Brandy." She replied with a shaky and unsure voice. I could tell she was crying.

"You're gonna come and live with me okay? Your sisters are with a family in Crosbyton. Me and Lonnie are gonna get them too, as soon as we can okay?" Cynthia said all in one go. "How soon?" I said in utter disappointment.

"As soon as we can, Brandy. Okay?" There was a long pause and so much heaviness in the air.

"Okay." I replied slowly but still having so many questions filling my head. "Where's my mom?".

"I don't know. Just hang out there at Onkas until I get there. I'm on my way, okay?" Cynthia said as she ended the call.

As a twelve-year-old, I didn't know exactly how long it took to get from the small Texas town of Andrews to Brownfield, but I knew it wouldn't take too long. I did just that, I sat and waited. Sitting in my soaking wet clothes in disbelief. *What was happening? Why when I leave to catch a break from that hell hole, did this have to happen? Why couldn't I have been there for my sisters? They must be so scared.* I thought in complete devastation. *I hate her... I HATE my mom.* The thought dropped in and sunk deep in my soul where I wanted it to stay. I was so angry at her. *How could she be so selfish and let this happen? I bet she left the girls at home alone and one of the girls got hurt,* I thought. Assumption after assumption filled my head as I sat waiting for my aunt to come and pick me up.

"You okay Brand?" Amber asked in helplessness.

"No. I'm not Amber. I miss my sisters. I should have been there." I bluntly responded. She just sat there next to me in silence with no response. There were no words. Finally, after what it seemed to be hours, my aunt Cynthia walked through the living room door. I ran to her, threw myself in her arms, and just cried my eyes out. I was so scared.

"It's gonna be okay Brand. Don't worry." She tried to confidently assure me as she held me tight for a few seconds. "Go get your clothes so we can get on the road."

"I have them on." I said as I stood there. Looking at my semi dry clothes in confusion, then looking at Veronica.

"It's all she came with." Veronica told her.

Cynthia looked back down at me with pure empathy. I could feel her heart go out to me. But I only felt embarrassed. I almost said I was sorry for not having any clothes. But I just ignored the thought, hugged Amber and walked outside toward my aunts' tan minivan. And within a few minutes' time, we were off to my new home in Andrews. Without my sisters.

CHAPTER

Seven

In Andrews, adjusting to my aunt Cynthia and Uncle Lonnie's house was almost easy. I had my three cousins to hang out with: Matthew, Miranda and closest to my age, Ashley. There was a meal prepared every night, their house was kept clean, and they did family things like watch movies together and play outside. I mean, I had stayed the night there with my cousin Ashley many times when we used to live in Andrews with my mom. So, it wasn't as if this was all new. At the same time, it was definitely different because I then lived there. I wasn't going back to my mom's house.

At the time, I could deal without seeing my mom. I held onto anger toward her longer than I realized. Yes,

I would catch myself trying to miss her but would remember everything and resist the urge. There was just one and very important thing I went to bed every night crying myself to sleep in secret about; and that was my sisters. My helpless sisters that I knew were probably scared and confused, wondering where they were and why. Scared that they would never see me or our mom again. It was a deep nagging pain in my broken heart that made the previous wounds dull and numb. A welcome distraction from the thought of my sisters was my nervousness of starting school.

Though every school I had transferred to throughout my dysfunctional, inconsistent and unstable childhood was never an easy start, they were all elementary schools. The little kids' schools. Now was the time for the big kid school, middle school. All of the fears of a twelve-year-old girl came flooding in. *What clothes do I wear? How do I fix my hair? I wonder if I'll make friends. What if nobody likes me?* Again, all of the fear. However, a bit of that fear was eased when my aunt and uncle took me school shopping. It wasn't the norm one pair of jeans and three shirts from the Family Dollar. It was shoes from Payless, clothes from the mall and school supplies from Walmart! That was so exciting to me. I was sure to meet friends with those cool clothes and school supplies. To my surprise, it wasn't long before it was the first day of sixth grade.

I was ready. I remember that due to me being a new student, I had to sit in the library for a few periods while my records, schedule and things were situated along with other students who had similar situations. As I sat, I thought *wow, I'm in middle school.* In awe, observing what I thought was the most enormous library I had ever been in. However, a white binder slamming down in front of me pulled me out of my thoughts. The binder had pictures tucked into the front plastic, it was now sitting on the table I was alone at.

"Wassup! I'm Lizzie. Well my real name is Elizabeth, but I go by Lizzie. What's your name?" She said so giddy, as she made herself comfortable in the seat next to mine.

Where did this girl even come from? She had long curly light brown, almost reddish hair, a light skin tone, slim and I could tell she stood a few inches taller than me. Her smile was bright and so welcoming. I immediately felt a sense of friendliness.

"Brandy... my name is Brandy. I'm new here." I replied.

"Oh snap, no way! Where'd you come from?" she questioned back at me.

"Denver City." I replied.

"Oh, for real? Where's that?" She said in wonder. "Honestly, I don't know? I just know it's probably

like an hour or so from here".

"Well that's wassup. Welcome to this sorry town called Andrews." She said within a giggle. We sat in that library together for close to an hour. We meshed so well. It was like a friend sent right to me. Before we both were called out to begin our scheduled day, Lizzie thankfully asked the golden question.

"Hey, wanna sit together at lunch? You'll have to meet my homegirl Makayla."

"Yeah... sure!" I exclaimed, trying to hide my excitement; so thankful I would have someone to sit with that I actually knew.

"Aight coo, I'll look for you." Then we went about our way and day. From that day forward, Lizzie and Makayla unknowingly made my life so much easier. Lizzie cracked me up every time I was with her, she helped bring out a sense of humor that I hadn't tapped into since I last hung out with my hilarious best friend Taylor from Denver City. Makayla was always keeping us in line because us two together were two goofballs always cracking jokes and could never take life seriously. My aunt and uncle would allow me to go over to their houses every now and then. I was so thankful for those two. Not very many other kids had much interest in getting to know or hang out with me. I understood I wasn't cool enough for the "popular rich girls", but I didn't mind. I had found my crowd and was absolutely fine with it. I was accepted.

About two months into school, I still had trouble with seeing the overhead projector and whatever else the teachers would teach on the marker board. I never mentioned it to my aunt or uncle, never wanting to burden them with my troubles. I felt that it was enough for them to take care of and allow me to live with them. Never mind having them buy me glasses. I simply became used to not being able to see so well. However, there was one special day where I'll never forget what happened.

A voice came on the intercom during my math lesson, "Can we have Brandy Tijerina come to the office please."

I sort of freaked out for a second thinking what did I do to be called to the office? I go, and to my sweet surprise, the office assistant handed me my glasses case with my glasses in them!

"A lady dropped these off for you. She said you'd need them and to give you this as well." The office assistant said to me.

It was a note written on yellow notepad paper that read a little something like *Sweet Brandy, it breaks my heart to know the things you have been through. But as I pray for you, I truly feel in my heart that God has you in His hands and has a very special plan for you. Keep sharing that beautiful smile and spirit you have. Always know I'm praying for you. Your teacher, Mrs.Williams.* I was floored. My sweet, loving and caring teacher from Denver City took time to find out where I was and drove out of her way to bring me the glasses that she bought me and knew how badly I would need them in school. That act of love was a love that I had never experienced. I could hear her soothing voice in my head as I read that note ove and over. I kept that note for many years and would read it when I'd feel discouraged. After many moves, after my Aunt and Uncles, I lost it in the rubble.

The best parts of living with my Aunt and Uncle, other than receiving structure, discipline, learning to do chores and having a bedtime, is that I began to love school again. I began to truly acclimate to this new life there in Andrews. I was introduced to athletics where I fell in love with exercise, I learned to play the trumpet and was actually pretty good at it if I do say so myself. While I did sleep in my aunt and uncles eight by seven laundry room, I loved it. I had my own, clean twin size bed tucked perfectly against a wall facing the washer and dryer. Why would I love that? It was safe, warm, clean and the smell of clean laundry was a constant scent in there. As I look back as an adult now, I think about how the most basic things that happened at my aunt and uncles meant the world to me. A consistent ride to and from school every day, my uncle saying no to me when I asked to go to a birthday party at a bar, having the chore of helping with dishes after dinner each night, having to keep up with my homework. Things that would normally get on a child's nerves were the very things my young soul yearned for. Structure, discipline, love, consistency. It was nice. It was a fall afternoon when the absolute best event happened.

I waited for my aunt to come and pick me up from school. While waiting, I sat in complete contentment of how life was now, except that I was starting to miss my mom. Despite her faults, at the end of the day, she was my mom. I would wonder how and where she was. As my aunt pulled up and interrupted the thought, I couldn't help but notice a big smile on her face as she parked in front of me. I hopped in with curiosity.

"So, I have a surprise for you." She said with glee in her voice. I looked back and all around in wonder of what she was talking about. I don't know that I ever had a good surprise in my life.

"What? What is it?" I said.

"It's at the house." She gleefully replied. I didn't know how to respond. I just sat there trying not to show my excitement as we drove home. We pulled up to her peach stucco three bedroom, one-bathroom house and I slowly got out, unsure of what to do.

"Well come on!" She said with an ear to ear smile.

I entered through the back door, walked through the laundry room/my bedroom and I couldn't believe my eyes. It was my sisters playing in the living room. My young heart leaped out of my chest as I ran to them, scooped them in my arms and wailed sobbing. Me and Alexis shared the tears of joy together while Jasmine was still too young to know what was going on. I knew in my heart she was happy to see her big sissy too though. My life couldn't be more complete at that moment. There we all were. Together again under one roof. What a blessing it was to my soul.

"Are they here to stay?" I asked my aunt and uncle, wiping my happy tears with hope.

"Yup. They're here to stay." My uncle said with pride and joy as he and my aunt smiled down at us.

I was so grateful for them. I know it wasn't easy for them. They had three kids of their own, took in three that weren't theirs under a small roof. *How generous and open hearted could someone be?* Again, I was grateful. As life continued to unfold gracefully, the holidays came around. It was Thanksgiving Day and I had already had my second plate, stuffed to the core like I always did. Never knowing what portions meant. I decided to watch Lifetime once my Uncle Lonnie's football game was over. I loved Lifetime. Murder, rape, drama, it infatuated me.

A movie about a ballerina was on. She was doing everything she could to make the star role in a ballet but couldn't meet the weight requirements. Out of frustration, she asked the girl who was given the role how she was able to meet such high demanding weight requirements.

The girl responded "easy, you eat whatever you want, then just stick your finger down your throat and you'll never gain a pound."

That sentence right there shut my whole world down. I was teased as a little girl for being overweight by family and boys on the playground. I had no idea about proper nutrition, was 4'10 and weighed close to 150lbs when I was first called fatty, pumpkin and such. I then realized my weight wasn't like other girls. I didn't know how to fix it, and it secretly bothered me every day. That Thanksgiving Day I began my downfall of silently suffering through 9 years of bulimia. It was a long, lonely and gloomy road.

The school year went on, and along the way of band practice, house chores, consistent dinners, and looking forward to school each day knowing I was actually going to finish the school year at one school, I was invited to a church by a sweet girl that I had also become friends with. Most times you could catch me with Lizzie and Makayla. When I wasn't around those two crazy-in-the-best-way girls, I was with sweet Ella.

I liked being around Ella. I could relate to her when it came to be having to take care of siblings. She was so kindhearted, selfless and soft spoken. I met her in band. She played the flute and I played the trumpet. She had invited me to a church multiple times, promising it wasn't weird. That it was just a place to go learn about Jesus.

I remembered learning a few things about the guy when I was a little girl and when my mom sent me to Vacation Bible School, we'd go to that Spanish church, or when my friend Summer, back in Denver City would invite me to GA's which stood for Girls In Action. Which I would only go to for the snacks and to hang out with her. Now here Ella was trying to get me to go to this thing called Youth. Why was this Jesus person talked about everywhere I went? Whatever, she promised it wouldn't be weird and that there would be boys, so I asked my aunt and uncle to go and boom, there I was once again sitting in a class hearing about Jesus. Of course, he didn't have my attention though. There was a guy who was an upperclassman in school; he certainly had my attention.

"Jordan is so fine Ella!" I admitted.

"Brandy!" She said with shock. "He's a senior silly?!"
"So? I've caught him looking at me too." I said.

Hoping I wasn't crazy; and I wasn't. I always looked forward to Wednesdays. By the time I knew it, I was sneaking out of my aunts back door in the middle of the night to go and see him. It was the way he looked at me. He saw me and gave me attention that I didn't know I desperately craved. Each time I would go to see him at night, I knew I was doing wrong. But I didn't care. A boy liked me. An older boy, which is what made it even more exciting in my mind. I felt so special. Even though he would have his girlfriend at church with him. Of course, it bothered me inside, but I never said anything or wanted to show it in fear that he would stop talking to me. I knew no one could know, and I was okay with that. Every dirty thing the other men had ever done to me wasn't known. So, what difference did this make? Things never went the whole nine yards, but the thought of me having an older boy's attention like this in sixth grade brought me a high that I began to think about daily.

Just like everything else, it came to an end. Sixth grade was almost over, Jordan was about to graduate, and me and my friends were ready for summertime! Until my aunt and uncle had to give the bad news. After finding out that baby number four was on her way, they had to make the tough decision of giving us up to the foster care system. I understood. Seven kids under one three-bedroom roof was a whole lot to handle. I was still grateful for the time we had there in Andrews. Sucked it up, tucked my feelings, and prepared for yet another move.

CHAPTER

Eight

It was only a day after sixth grade had ended that we were headed to a foster home in Brownfield, Texas. My aunt, with defeat in her voice, told me that we were going to a foster home, but that didn't change the love and respect I had for her and my uncle for taking us in and doing their best for as long as they could. Then as my mind wondered about Brownfield, it wasted no time rushing to memories of being a little girl there with my mom. But I had hope of going somewhere safe this time, to where I pushed those memories down in my soul as if they were just a bad dream. At least I had my sisters with me. At least we were being placed together, and at least we were going to a town where things weren't brand new. And while I definitely was sad to say goodbye to my friends that I had met and grew close to, I had already grown to become content with moving and saying bye to friends without grieving too badly. I promised I would call them from my new house number as soon as I was settled. Eventually, the day came. My caseworker Nicole stood at the doorway of my aunt Cynthia and Uncle Lonnie's house as me and my sisters placed each of our few bags of clothes right by her waiting for instructions.

"Alright, are we ready?" She said with a warm smile. She looked like a fairly young Hispanic woman. I found her to be pretty. I had only met her a time or two for our visits. Where she came to make sure that my sisters and I were doing okay.

"Well, let's get moving!" She exclaimed. We each grabbed our bags, my aunt grabbed Jasmines, and we made our way to Nicole's white two door Ford truck. We saddled up, cried a few tears, said goodbye to our family, and off we were to Brownfield. It wasn't too long of a drive. The girls fell asleep safely in the back seat to the soft country music Nicole put on and allowed me to get lost in my thoughts. *What kind of house will we live in? Will I have my own room? Are these people Hispanic like us?* After wondering for about an hour or so, the Brownfield City Limit sign came across my sight. Just like that I was back in a town where all I seen was darkness as a child. Again, never mind that. *Don't think about it Brandy. You'll be fine. It'll be different this time.* I thought to myself.

"How do you feel? Are you ready?" Nicole asked.

"Okay, I guess. I don't know." Which was very much true. I felt safe but felt numb all in one. I didn't know

how to feel. Anytime I would allow myself to feel, I would get angry and tears would fill my eyes. Feelings were something I didn't often feel like experiencing.

We made our way through the small town, made a few turns here and there, then ended up in a rich neighborhood, or so how I viewed it as. My definition of rich was brick houses and green grass. Any house I had ever lived-in before my aunts was definitely not brick and had a messy yard with dead grass. My heart honestly got excited to be driving in that neighborhood. Then, as Nicole began to slow down and park in front of a (in my opinion at the time) huge sized redbrick house with green grass on Harris St, I locked my eyes on our new home.

I paused for a good second, trying my best to grasp the fact that we were about to start living with complete strangers. Nicole stared at me waiting for a reaction.

"You okay?" she asked me. "Yeah..." I slowly replied.

"Alright, well let's go meet the Thompsons. Jasmine, Alexis... are ya'll ready?" She said gently waking my sisters.

"Is this our new house Brand?" Alexis asked as she raised her head to look out of her window.

"Yep. What do you think?" I asked her, trying to sound confident.

"It's big!" She said with excitement.

I knew Alexis wasn't scared. She always knew that if I was with her, she would be safe. Anytime I would sense that she felt safe with me, were the times I felt the most scared. I dared not show it though. I never wanted my sisters to fear losing me again or them being in danger.

"Well, let's get out so we can see the inside of your new home!" Nicole opened her truck door and opened the back door to let my sisters out.

We each walked together and approached the front door with our bags in hand, Jasmines hand in my free hand. *Wow, a doorbell.* I thought once Nicole gave it a ring. Shortly after the ding dong, a simple looking white woman, with straight short light brown hair wearing a blue country sundress with sunflowers printed on it came swiftly to the door to greet us.

"Hello there!" She said with a bright smile.

I caught a safe vibe from her the moment she looked at me with her warm light brown eyes. She gently welcomed us in and led us through their bland living room passing dark floral couches into their dull dining room. We sat at a roomy dark oak wood oval table and stared at an old Oakwood china cabinet with porcelain dishes, as Nicole and Kimberly casually conversed from across the table for about ten minutes. Until we heard a voice that traveled from the kitchen.

"Howdy!" Tod Thompson exclaimed with glee. He marched into the dining room, smiling from ear to ear. Also, white, wearing wide and light blue jeans with a dark brown leather belt wrapped around his belly button space. Red and black, short sleeve button up shirt. He had straight short and thin brown hair swooped to the left of his forehead. I immediately decided I didn't like him. Maybe it was my instant distrust of men, but I decided it and stuck to it. My guard went all the way up in an instant toward him. I did what I always knew to do, fake it.

"I'm Tod!" he said loudly.

"I'm Alexis!" My sister said without hesitation. "Very nice to meet you, Alexis. And you must be

Brandy. The oldest sister, right?" Tod said, his eyes turned towards me.

"Yeah." I said with no face expression.

He smiled. "Well hi there Jasmine. Aren't you the cutest thing? I'm so glad y'all are here. How was the drive?" He turned his attention to Nicole.

"Not too bad." Nicole responded. "The girls took a nice nap so they should be good to go for the rest of the day."

"Well good! Girls, would y'all like to see y'all's rooms?" Tod asked. No one responded.

"Sure, they do!" Nicole answered for us, trying to break the hard ice that sat heavily in the dining room.

"Alrighty then! Come right on back." Tod said. We all followed Tod across the kitchen and through a hallway. The first room he showed was mine. I didn't want to show how excited I was that I would be able to have my own room, but deep down my heart was gleaming. The girls would share a room just down the hall from me which made me feel at ease. "Brody should be home any minute from school. It's the last day of school, so summer is almost officially here." Tod said, trying to strike a friendly conversation.

"Brody?" I blurted with confusion. Nicole and Tod made eye contact. "I figured I would allow you to introduce him." Tod nodded with an understanding.

"Brody is also living here. He is finishing up with his third-grade year. He's a very sweet kid. I think y'all will get along just fine." Tod explained. It felt so weird. I remember thinking *is this real? Am I really about to live here?* Before that thought could be processed, Nicole began to make her dismissal.

"Well alright then. It looks like my work here is done… for today at least. Brandy, can I speak to you privately please?" Thankfully she asked because I started to freak out a bit internally. We made our way outside and stood on Tod and Kimberly's porch.

"How do you feel sweetheart? I know this is a lot, but the Thompsons are a great couple. They have been fostering for a couple of years now and we have never had an issue." Nicole tried to reassure me.

"I just don't like him." I said honestly.

Nicole giggled. "Ohh sweetheart. I understand. But I assure you, you are safe. Give it some time and this could turn out to be a good thing. Okay?".

"I guess." I said with annoyance. After our short pep talk, we made our way back inside so that Nicole could say bye to each of us and was on her way.

"Go unpack your things." I told Alexis; Jasmine simply followed. I headed for my new room and sat on the corner of the bed. I looked around and didn't know how to feel. *Was I scared? Sad? Confused? I didn't know.* All I knew was to tune out how I felt and just start unpacking. Shortly after Nicole left, Kimberly and Tod knocked on my open door.

"Brandy, this is Brody." There stood a short, petite, sweet looking boy with bleach blonde hair.

"Hey." I said, not knowing what else to say. "Hey," He said back, also feeling awkward.

"Brandy is thirteen, Brody. Isn't that cool? We have a teenager in the house now." Tod said. Brody didn't seem too thrilled, but I could relate. So, I definitely was not offended.

"So, where's your room?" I asked. "In the attic." He replied.

"Yeah, he's got his own boy cave up there, don't you Brody?" Tod butted in.

"Yeah, I guess." Brody shrugged.

Once we were introduced, I went back to unpacking and could hear them introducing my sisters. It was about sunset and as I slowly unpacked my last bag, all I could think about was food. DING DONG!

"Ah, the pizza is here!" I heard Kimberly say from the kitchen. "Oh my gosh, yes. Pizza!" I thought. Not knowing when to walk out of my room. Still feeling like I was in a complete stranger's house not knowing what moves to make. "Knock knock, you hungry? We got pizza!" Tod stood at my doorway with a friendly smile. Without responding, I stopped unpacking, slowly rose, and headed toward the kitchen. My sisters were already sitting at the kitchen bar when I entered.

"Look Brand! We get to have pizza!" My six-year- old energetic sister cheerfully exclaimed. "Kimberly usually cooks supper, but we thought tonight was a special night. So, we got three kinds of pizza that we hope y'all will like." Tod was trying. I could tell, but it was only day one, and if he thought I was going to trust him that easy, he thought wrong. Boy was he and Kimberly in for it with me.

CHAPTER

Nine

It was summer of 2006, and as I familiarized myself with the neighborhood, I also began to learn that I no longer had to be so guarded over my sisters. Kimberly and Tod seemed to have had experience with young ones to where both my sisters could easily be around them and Brody. It did enlighten me knowing they were comfortable and began to feel safe without me always being right there, but as for myself, I wouldn't give the Thompsons much of a chance. All I wanted to do was be in my room, door shut with Mariah Carey, Ashanti, or the newest hip hop and R&B artist playing while I laid there talking to Lizzie or Makayla on the house phone. Or get lost in my thoughts of my mom, wondering where and how she was. Or about how if I was still in Andrews, if Jordan would have ever left his girlfriend for me.

Most days, when the sun would go down, I'd go for a run at a walking park down the street to relieve stress of seventh grade that was coming up. Yes, another school. But not just any school, another middle school. I didn't want to start getting fat again, or so I would tell myself. So, purging after dinner and running wasn't an option for me. It was almost a full year into not allowing my body to digest much of what I ate and would make myself sick. Promising myself that I would never be called fat again. That summer, I thankfully happened to meet a girl named Tanika while shooting hoops alone at Colonial Heights, the elementary school around the corner. I learned that she too would slip away from her house to go and just be alone at that playground. We started to meet almost daily, and it lifted some stress knowing that we got along so well, and that she was going to the eighth grade. We'd be going to the same school together so thank goodness I would know someone.

As we continued our meetups, there would also be boys that would walk over to the park from time to time. One of the boys I had begun crushing on. He happened to be someone I remembered from a place my mom and stepdad would take us back when they were together. Before Denver City or Seagraves. Now there we were a little older. Both in middle school, except he would be in Tanika's grade, the grade above me, the grade I should have been going to as well.

But never mind that. He and another boy would meet there often. Even when Tanika couldn't meet me, I always made my way there knowing my crush would be there.

One fine sunny afternoon, there at the playground, it ended up just being him and I that met up. He invited me over to his house explaining that his parents weren't home. I remember feeling butterflies as well as a huge gut feeling that I shouldn't. And to be honest, the only reason I felt that I shouldn't was the fear of my foster dad, Tod, driving around there and realizing I wasn't there. My rebellion began to rise that summer, and I wasn't afraid of the feeling. There I went, off to his house that was in the neighborhood of the elementary school. I walked in and stood inside the doorway to his living room.

"Do you want a coke?" He asked, walking toward his kitchen.

"Nah I'm alright." I replied. He came back into the living room.

"Why do you look scared? Sit down crazy girl." He giggled softly. I felt safe, I wanted to be there. I was just freaking out that I was at a boy's house with no one around. I sat down next to him on the couch and watched him play his video game for a bit. Once he lost a few times, he gave up and turned the game off.

"So, what do you wanna do?" He asked with curiosity, leaning in closer into my bubble, staring me in the eyes.

"I don't know... what do you wanna do?" I said shyly, doing the same.

"This." He leaned in and his lips connected to mine.

I didn't mind, I began to apply everything I learned from all of the times I made out with Jordan back in Andrews. Hot feelings began to take over as we continued our make out session. He stood up and asked if I wanted to go to his room. I knew what would happen if I did. But I wanted to. All the times I wanted to do the same with Jordan to prove I was worthy to be liked, or maybe even loved by a boy, but it never happened. But here was the chance. A chance to be able to experience this level of intimacy unforced. With a guy I actually liked. I stood up and allowed him to lead me to his bedroom.

I was thirteen years old when I willingly lost my virginity. No, we had no clue what we were doing, but it felt good to feel wanted by someone I found attractive and my age. More than anything, I wanted him to like me and maybe even make me his girlfriend. So, if this was the way, then I didn't mind at all. I walked home after it happened, and as I walked, I remember my mind racing *why don't I feel good about this? Does he still like me? He didn't say much afterwards. What if I wasn't good enough for him? I wonder if he'll be at the park tomorrow.*

"Howdy!" Tod exclaimed as I walked in the door. "You hungry?". Annoyed at the sound of his voice, I made no eye contact.

"Nah not really." I replied as I walked past him, heading straight for my room to think about what had just happened. I tossed and turned that night, not being able to sleep. Hoping that the boy would be at Colonial the next day. Once I woke up, I went about my normal day's routine of staying in my room, listening to music, and only going out to eat breakfast and lunch. After lunch, I swiped heavy coats of mascara on, sprayed my hair with hairspray until it was crunchy, put on my shortest t-shirt shorts I had and told Tod and Kimberly I was headed to Colonial to hang out with Tanika.

"Can I come too Brand? Please?" Alexis asked. "Next time, Lex." I told her.

"You said that yesterday!" She pouted.

"Oh my gosh, whatever. Don't ask again or I won't ever let you come, period." I snapped at her. Tod and Kimberly really never knew how to approach me, and I sensed it. They never butted in when Alexis and I had our little moments. I liked that I was gaining control of my life in small ways like that one.

"Alright, just try to be back before supper okay?" Kimberly gently asked.

"Sure, Kim." I smiled and left. Heart pounding as I approached the playground where we would usually meet, he wasn't there.

"Hey, wassup! I called you yesterday, but your foster dad said you was here at the park. I came and you weren't here?" Tanika said while approaching me.

"Man, I just needed to walk. I didn't feel like being around nobody." I said while looking around the park.

"Oh okay..." She said with a blank stare. We both stuck around for a while just talking, but at the back of my head all I could think about was my crush not showing up. When that day was over, I went the next day, and the next, and nothing. I was so hurt. At times I wanted to go knock on his front door to see if he could come to the playground, but I never gained the courage. I couldn't take the secret anymore, I had to tell someone, so I spilled the beans to Tanika hoping she wouldn't freak out on me.

"No, you didn't! Brandy, he has a girlfriend!" She said in shock. My heart sank when she said those words.

"He does? Don't play Tanika."

"I put that on my momma. She's in the same grade as me. Her name is Sophia. They been dating since the sixth grade." she told me in earnest. I couldn't believe it. The first guy I willingly gave my virginity to had a girlfriend.

"Man, I really thought he liked me. Please don't say anything Tanika." I begged her.

"I won't, promise. I won't do you like that, but you better hope he don't tell his best friend Nico though.

That boy has a mouth." She read the worry on my face.

"Don't trip girl, if anyone tries to say anything, I got your back." Tanika vowed to me.

"Thanks." I said with regret in my heart.

School was only a week and a half away, and I was not ready. I was going to be the new girl that was a foster child, who gave her virginity to a guy who had already had a girlfriend. What a great start. Why was it a good idea at the time but came to be a nightmare all around. My nerves ran hot as the first day quickly approached. I contemplated for an hour on what to wear. It had to be perfect. Once the perfect outfit was chosen, onto my hair I went.

As I thoroughly sprayed my wet hair with Tresemmé hairspray, I was beginning to vaguely hear a noise that didn't rub me the right way. I turned down my soft song I was listening to and realized it was my sister Alexis crying.

I quickly made my way down the hall and into their room to find my foster mom being just a little too aggressive with her, shoving a shirt on her while squeezing her arm. I rapidly went in for Kimberly's arm and grabbed it aggressively.

"Don't you EVER put your hands on either of my sisters." I said with a bold tone while rage raised in my blood and looking her dead in her eyes.

"I'm sorry Brandy, she just wasn't listening to me, and I was just trying to get her dressed. I don't want y'all to be late." Kimberly calmly said to me.

"I don't care Kimberly. Just don't. Alexis, put your freaking clothes on and don't make me tell you again." I snapped at both of them. My sister quickly did as I said. I remember having somewhat of a strong will to protect them. I knew my sisters still viewed me as a mother like sister and I would rather be the one to get stern with them then see strangers do so. My heart couldn't take that, and Kimberly thankfully understood.

It was off to school we went. Lucky me, Tod was the sixth-grade computer teacher, and apparently, he made the announcement to his students on the last day of school, the school year prior, about how he was going to be fostering a girl that would be in their grade the upcoming year. Yes, I quickly realized that fact as I quietly went through my first day thinking no one would realize I was that girl. Hoping I was simply a new girl, non-more. The school outline was a bit different from Andrews Middle School, but the students seemed the same as far as style and school supplies trends, so I at least had that going for me. I struck a short conversation or two here and there, then lunch time came about. I thankfully saw a familiar face and headed for her direction. It was a girl that lived down the street from me, that I had nothing in common with but found that she was polite and open during the summer. With ease she welcomed me to a seat, and we enjoyed our lunch. Instead of going outside after lunch, I stayed in the restroom knowing the eighth graders would be out there. God forbid I see my old crush. I had yet to see Tanika. All I knew was that once anyone found out about my secret, it wouldn't take long to get around that small school.

The rest of the day was smooth, no real conversations; but I didn't mind. Until volleyball practice. About a month before school had started, Tod had asked if I was interested in playing sports. Remembering how much I fell in love with athletics in Andrews, I said yes without hesitation. Which is what led me to again, volleyball practice after the first day of school.

"Hi! I'm Jessica!" A small, preppy white girl with braces and glasses, with light brown hair and brown eyes abruptly introduced herself as I stepped foot onto the court, waiting for everyone else to finish dressing so we could get tryouts started.

"Uh... I'm Brandy." I said with a shy tone and halfway smile. This chick was a happy soul. Different. I didn't know what it was, but I almost instantly drew to her.

"Cool! ... Wait, Brandy as in Mr. Thompson's foster daughter Brandy?!" My heart sank, how did she know this?

"Yeah..." The look on my face is what asked the question, I'm sure.

"Oh wow, I knew we were going to have a new girl. He told us last year that he would be fostering a girl in our grade named Brandy. I just remembered when you said your name, I'm sorry, I hope that wasn't rude?" she said to me. I was more embarrassed than anything. I didn't want to be known as the foster kid. But it was my reality so, I guess I had to learn to deal with it.

"It's all good. It's nice to meet you Jessica." I said.

"Oh, just call me Jess." She said with the biggest smile that I couldn't tell was fake for as much enthusiasm she had or actually real. Nevertheless, I decided I liked her. After Jessica, all the other girls began to introduce themselves. They all made me feel so welcome. I'll never forget how accepted I felt the first day at Brownfield Middle School. I had never had so much attention in my life. Day after day of that first week of school, I felt that I had a lot of boys notice me that were in my grade, and so many girls wanted to be my friend. *What was this?* In all of my previous schools, I was just another face in the crowd. The chubby girl with stinky clothes that always squinted, or the girl that wore lots of hairspray and baggy clothes with three, maybe four friends. I didn't know what it was, but I loved it.

I never once thought I was pretty or cool, but the students at Brownfield Middle School thought otherwise. Despite the fact that the eighth graders found out about me giving it up to their classmate that

had a girlfriend, I finally felt cool and became popular. Within that first week I had a boyfriend. He was a football player and a tough guy. Now, what having a boyfriend in middle school meant was that he would walk you to your classes after every period, sit with you at lunch, and call your house phone after school to sit and breath over the phone together. Yeah, it was really a thing. It wasn't long before I became bored with that boyfriend and wanted a boyfriend that would at least kiss me. Then after having a boyfriend that would kiss me, maybe it wouldn't be a huge deal if I had a boyfriend that would do more than kiss. After all, I knew what it was to go all the way, and if I wanted to stay popular and feel seen and wanted, I should probably keep that up.

"Brandy..." Tod approached me and began walking beside me as I was on my way to English. He stared right at the hickey I had on my neck. In which I thought it was cute and made me feel marked and wanted. "You don't want to be known as the school slut, do you?" He said in a taunting tone. Before I smart mouthed back, I did my best to ignore him, rolled my eyes and walked off. He didn't understand.

CHAPTER

Ten

To add some sunshine, as the school year flew on by, I learned something new about myself that year; I liked to write. My English teacher, Mrs. Downs would give us random topics to write on. She then would have me wait after class to affirm me in being a writer.

"I'm going to have you attend the advanced English class next year Brandy. I see your love for reading and writing. Keep that up." She once said.

I'll never forget it. I maintained my friends and made plenty more. By the end of the year I was friends with almost half of my grade and had favor with lots of boys.

Even some of the eighth-grade boys from them finding out what I did with one of their classmates. Thus, I did stay with one particular boy for a little while. More than any other boyfriend I had that year. He was a bad boy. Cussed, talked back to teachers, liked to fight, and other boys feared him. His mom wasn't a part of his life, and his dad was in prison. He lived with his grandma in a small two-bedroom house that I got to know very well, when I would tell my foster parents I would be at a friend's house, but instead be at his. I felt comfortable being around him. He carried this demeanor of toughness that made me feel safe and lucky to be with him. I felt as if he understood me the most, so I gave my everything to him. I felt that I could be with him forever. Sadly, the attraction that he had for me didn't last long enough. After a couple months he was on to the next girl. There was my first heartbreak. I really felt for the boy. Again, I gave him everything he asked of me and yet it still wasn't enough to keep him. I remember comparing myself to the girl he cheated on me with, and eventually left me for. She was taller, skinnier, had already developed her boobs, and had straight hair. Meanwhile, when I looked in the mirror, I saw a short, chubby faced, curly haired girl that had no boobs. I felt as if that's why he left me. The constant voices in my head told me that my looks weren't good enough.

Even though I was doing my best to not allow too much food to settle in me to stay thinner, I still felt chubby. I didn't feel worthy and began to truly dislike who I was. While my seventh-grade year looked great on the outside with various activities such as playing all of the sports, making the best teams, having all of the friends, boy's attention, and I just made cheerleading for the next year.

Inside I was slowly crumbling in spirit. It was as if I felt a belonging, yet still alone.

It was late one night, about three weeks left in the school year. I sprawled out on my bed, falling fast asleep around the time I normally did on a school night. When suddenly I heard the house phone ring. My eyes shot open and heart thumped knowing I wasn't allowed phone calls after 9pm or Tod would answer and tell whoever to call back tomorrow in a somewhat rude tone. And that was always embarrassing. I waited a moment wondering if it was for me, then I heard a knock on my door.

"Brandy..." Tod opened my door and stood there. "Now, normally I wouldn't allow this, but this call seems important." He said with a tired look on his face. I was struck with confusion. *Who in the world?*

"Hello...?" I said, slowly.

"Brand... it's Makayla." My friend from Andrews said with a tight voice.

"Kaykay? What's the matter?" I said with the pitch rising in my voice.

"Lizzie..." She said, leaving me hanging.

"Lizzie? Where is she? What's wrong Kay?" I began to panic from the vibe she was sending through the

phone. I could just feel that something was severely wrong.

"She... she..." Still unable to say what was the matter because of the sobbing that had begun. "She passed away Brand...". My eyes widened and my heart sank simultaneously. I felt as if I lost my hearing for a second.

"What... Makayla, please tell me this is a joke. This isn't funny!" Tears began to fill my eyes.

"I'm sorry to tell you like this Brand... I wish you were here dude. She died. It was an accident, but she passed away." Her words were choppy in between her sobs. I couldn't believe what I was hearing. I was devastated and my heart broke into a thousand pieces. Her beautiful light skinned face ran across my memory. Her goofy laugh is all I could hear in my head. She was my first friend that made the first day of a really hard time easy. She accepted me before she ever knew me. It hit me hard and I just cried myself to sleep. I was fourteen and lost a person that I loved and was thankful for. It was a horrible feeling. All I kept thinking is how young she was, and with a blink of an eye she was gone. When I woke up the next morning, I wondered if it was a nightmare I had. I hoped it was until Tod asked if I wanted to stay home from school that day. I told him I'd be okay and went. I didn't want to be in my lonely room with her memory for that day. I needed to be around friends. I went off to school with puffy eyes and said my eyes were hurting if anyone asked. I told no one about Lizzie. I remember being at lunch, trying my best to eat something, then suddenly hearing her laugh in my head. I had food in my mouth and leaned my head down as tears began to fill my eyes. It was incredibly hard to swallow what was in my mouth.

"Brandy, are you okay?" My friend Brittney asked.

"Yeah, I'm gonna go to the bathroom." I dipped off and sat in a stall to release the tears that were burning to be released while remembering my dear friend, regretting not staying home. As much as I had enjoyed the new school life, I was so ready for summer. To where I would be able to choose when I wanted to see people and when I didn't. Especially when I felt that I couldn't explain the pain I had going on inside of me. Finally, summer had arrived. I was relieved; my friends and I were off to be the top dogs of the school. But before that, we had business to handle. That business was to enjoy the sunny season as best as we could in that ol' small town of Brownfield.

Late nights, sleepovers, prank calls, volleyball nights at the park, the pool, etc. I remember being at the sand courts, and my ex-boyfriend being there with his thug friends playing basketball across the way from us volleyball players. I'd catch him looking my way from time to time, and it flattered me. I made sure to pull my shorts up just a little more to keep his attention while playing my favorite sport with my friends. I thought that my body was the way to a guy's heart. Showing and giving him something to satisfy him before the next girl did. Always trying to prove myself worthy of love and affection. I wondered if he was still with that girl he left me for, but heck I didn't care. I still wanted his attention. And if I could win him back, I would be satisfied and maybe prove to myself that I was worthy. Once he caught me looking a few times too, he finally made his way to the volleyball court along with his friends.

"Wassup! Ya'll tryna get balled on?" he yelled over to us. All my friends knew why he went over, so almost naturally, his friends began to talk to mine before beginning our match, while leaving him and I alone to chat.

"Wassup… whatchu getting into tonight?" He asked softly, with his seductive tone that I missed so much. His thug demeanor always attracted me. How he looked at me made me feel wanted and desired. All I ever wanted to feel.

"I don't know... just hanging out I guess." I coyly replied.

"Oh yeah? You gonna let me swing through yo crib or what?" he said, jumping straight to his point. I immediately felt a blush come over me. I didn't even think to ask if he still had a girlfriend. Again, I didn't care.

"Yeah, come through around midnight, and I'll be outside waiting." I replied with a smile.

"Alright." he said with excitement. Knowing I would give him what he wanted if he really went.

"Let's go see what skills you have on this court." He said, walking away. We headed back into the crowd and began our game. I could barely focus on the fun we were having because I was trying to figure out how I could be outside at midnight to meet him. Tod and Kimberly had an alarm system to where if I opened any door, a quick *beep beep beep* would go off. As my mischievous mind began to brainstorm while bumping setting and spiking, the most spontaneous idea of having a sleepover came about. I mean it would be perfect since most of my friends were already there at the courts. If they stayed the night, I could just ask Tod if we could all sleep on the trampoline, where I could be outside for my ex. It was the perfect plan. There I went with my bossy attitude I picked up along the way of rarely hearing no, calling up my foster dad.

"Hey Tod, is it cool that I have a sleepover tonight? It'll be Kaitlyn, Erin, Brittney and Briana. We won't be loud." I asked. I could hear him breathe a deep irritated breath before he replied. "As long as it's okay with their parents." He said with a defeated tone.

"Okay!" I alerted the girls and they were up for it. Each friend cleared it with their parents, and we all piled into Tod's eight-seater white suburban when I called him back to come and pick us all up. When we arrived at our house, the girls got comfy in my room and I went to ask the golden question for the night.

"Tod, can we sleep on the trampoline?" I said with confidence.

"That's fine. Just keep it down so y'all don't wake the neighbors." He agreed. There we all were. Blankets and pillows sprawled across the trampoline as we giggled, told each other secrets, talked about crushes and so forth. Then when I felt it was about time that my ex showed up, I came out with the news.

"Alright guys, so Devon is coming to see me in a little bit." I told them with a smirk.

"What! Like, here? Oh my gosh Brandy!" Erin frantically said.

"Dude chill, Tod and Kimberly sleep hard. They won't wake up as long as we're not crazy loud." I retorted.

"If you say so." She blurted. I became so selfish when it came to boys. Boys that I had deep feelings for. The first boy to that extreme was Devon. The boy that I knew I could prove that I could be better than the girl he chose over me. It wasn't too much longer after I told the girls that we began to hear dogs barking down the alley. Then, like a thief in the night, we saw hands catch a grip onto the top of Tod's white tin metal fence, and Devon's face come up over it along with the rest of his body. After him came his two other friends. Two friends that I had no idea were coming too. I didn't ask questions because I didn't want him to leave if I did. They came over to the trampoline and made small talk with us girls. I could

see Devon scanning my backyard for a private place. There wasn't one.

"So wassupp, are we gonna be able to come inside or what?" he said, scanning the backyard.

"Uh, y... yeah. Let me just make sure Tod and Kimberly are still knocked out." I answered. Trying to hide the nervousness in my voice. If I was caught, it would be the first of something this extreme. Everything wrong I had ever done behind Tod and Kimberly's back was away from the house. At a friend's house, or park, or car. But for Devon, it was a risk I was willing to take. The girls tried to tell me it wasn't a good idea. But I was hardheaded and didn't want to listen to anyone but myself. We all maneuvered inside to the very back den. The furthest room from Tod and Kimberly's room. It was all fun and games for a bit, then my sister Alexis walked into the room and wanted to hang.

"Dude, go back to sleep Lex." I was annoyed with her presence.

"If I have to go back to sleep, then I'm waking up Tod." She whined back at me.

"Ugh... then just be quiet then, gahh." I snapped back at her. She made herself comfortable while scanning the room.

"I don't like you." She told Devon as soon as she looked his way. She caught me crying one night and asked why. I told her my boyfriend broke up with me and to leave me alone. I had previously shown her pictures of him, so she knew exactly who he was when she saw him.

"Good. I don't like you either." Devon didn't hesitate to respond.

"Oh my gosh, stop. Come with me." I grabbed Devon's hand and tugged on him until he got up to follow me. I led him to the front dining room where no one was and gave him what he went for, in hopes that maybe he would see that we could get back together. Shortly after, we laid there on the dining room floor as all of the others were still hanging out in the den. I did feel as if they were getting a little too loud if I could hear them, but it was when I heard my little sister say with a loud voice down the hallway

"Oh, hi Tod, HI TOD." She repeated herself a few times before I got the hint that Tod was awake and headed for the den.

"WHAT IN THE WORLD ARE Y'ALL DOING

IN MY HOUSE!" He yelled. My body froze. Me and Devon locked eyes in fear. I put my finger over my mouth signing for him to stay quiet. All while we heard a fuss of commotion, and the back door open, then slam.

"Brand, where are you?" I heard Brittney in a loud whisper. Devon and I quickly rose to our feet as Britt turned the corner. She looked at Devon and told him "you better leave now before he comes back. He left chasing your friends."

That was the cue to get him out fast. He slipped through the front door and I went into a slight panic all while trying to keep my cool. Needless to say, the cops were called, my friends were all sent home at about one thirty in the morning, and I was G-R-O- U-N-D-E-D. I'm talking door hinges taken off of my door, a baby monitor in my room, no phone, dishes after every meal, lawn mowed once a week and I was to go everywhere they went. I was no longer allowed to be at the house by myself for the rest of the summer; and no, Devon never wanted to date me again. Let's just say that summer did not go as planned.

Once eighth grade started, and I was no longer grounded. I did my best to not screw up again. At least not like that. That year, I was a cheerleader. I had to do my best in school and represent leadership. Whatever that meant. I'll always remember how a boy asked me out after a football game from across the football field as the cheer squad was sitting, having somewhat of a powwow on the empty field.

"BRANDY!!" His voice projected across the field and caught everyone's attention. "WILL YOU BE MY GIRL-FRIEND?!" I had always thought he was a cutie and so sweet, but he was my best friend Kory's relative. He was also a grade beneath me, seventh grade.

When he asked, I blushed. I found it to be so flattering. I looked over at Kory, asking with my eyes if I should say yes. She nodded yes with her cheerful smile and without hesitation.

"Say yes Bran!" She then exclaimed. I looked back over at the boys that were still in uniform headed for the locker room, including himself but standing there waiting for an answer. I didn't want to yell back, so I just gave a shy smile and a thumbs up from across the field. The way he was so excited that I said yes really made me feel something. Wanted, seen. All I ever craved. Our relationship actually lasted for the entire school year and summer. It was within that year when we dated that I began to really be a part of something that was foreign to me. I was over at his house quite a bit. Yet, instead of him wanting to sleep with me, he would want me to have dinner with him and his family or watch him and his older sister make Christian songs together. His family would pray before meals, listen to Christian music in their vehicles, take me to church with them, and began to tell me that they loved me before long. At first, I never knew how to respond. I mean, the way he and they treated me was out of this world. I had never seen or felt what it meant to be respected and cherished until him. When I was sick, he'd show up at my door-step just to drop off ice cream, say he's praying for my health, then run back to his dad's truck as his dad waved at me with a smile, then drove off. He noticed that I was always wearing hand me downs from friends, or simply used clothes from the Children's Home so he would ask his dad for small jobs to earn money to buy me clothes.

That year, on Valentine's Day, we went to dinner at a church. After, his parents picked us up, took us to their house, and watched their son get on his knee to give me a promise ring. I was undone. I had never in my life felt so loved. I felt as if I was in a dream. It wasn't real. That if he really knew who I was and where I came from, he wouldn't feel that way about me anymore. I was always on edge ready for him to leave me for someone better. Some-one he truly deserved. Not some used up foster girl from the hood. But he never did. Then, when summer came to a closure and school was about to start, I began to worry. It was going to be hard with my boyfriend staying in middle school as I headed for the big house. But I would be crazy to mess things up, right? However, I did. I ruined what was the best thing that had happened to me.

It wasn't long after school started that I began to get Senior boys' attention. My boyfriend's older sister was a Senior as well, so I couldn't show any signs of interest in them of course, but deep down I was. It was bad boys that had my full attention. Before long, I was back to my old ways of giving my body to them. I didn't know why I did it at the time. I would even ask myself *Brandy, what are you doing.* I would also think, *what he doesn't know won't hurt.* Until one day, his sister came to pick me up for school. On the way there, she turned her radio down and asked, "so, what happened with you and my brother?"

"W..what do you mean?" I stuttered back.

"Well, he said you broke up with him. He's pretty upset, and I was just wondering why you did? What happened?" she asked me. I was shocked. I didn't break up with him. I was so confused. Until it hit me, he knew. I don't know how, but I knew he had to know. When I got out of volleyball practice that day, I called him. No answer. I called him for days after that, and still no answer. He straight up cut me out of his whole world.

I remember how regret rained all over me. Especially knowing that this one particular guy I was messing around with didn't want a relationship. Just a playmate, basically. However, part of me felt relieved that my boyfriend had ended it with me. I never believed I deserved him anyway.

Then the other part of me always missed him and how he loved and treated me.

I began to feel alone all over again. I would mask frustration with sex and partying on the weekends when I was supposed to be staying at friends' houses. I began to make a bad reputation for myself with the guys. Lots of times the main guy I would mess around with, Bobby, would pick me up in his old school blue Chevy and take me to Senior parties or his house and I'd go home smelling like weed. Tod asked what the smell was, and I'd just shrug and go to my room until the next day when I'd come out for food fueling up for the next day. I began sneaking out of my window quite a bit to go and see him. If it wasn't to see him, it was to go and party. Just being back before dawn is what was always in my head. Until one night of getting busted then grounded again, and again and again for more wild acts. I became out of control. A promiscuous liar and thief. Even pierced my own tongue with a sewing needle and carved my mom's name in my inner ankle. No matter what Tod and Kimberly did, they couldn't hold me down. I grew the mentality that if anyone disrespected me, fight them. I always figured out how to have it my way. If I didn't have my way, then I'd raise hell. I'll always remember how one of my classmates/friends, Monica, who is now one of my three best friends, would randomly walk up to me and say "Brandy, I'm praying for you. Believe me when I say God has a plan for you."

It almost annoyed me because thinking about my life and how God would allow it, but oddly made me feel some type of comfort as well. One day, Tod caught and picked me up at my aunt's house, a place where I loved to hang out with my cousin Amber. A place that was completely safe and stable, only seven blocks away from Tod and Kimberly's house, but I wasn't allowed to be at according to CPS regulations. It was as if every rule became more intense and ridiculous once we received a new case investigator about a year prior.

"Brandy, if you keep breaking the rules and doing what you're doing, you're going to end up like your mom. Opening your legs to anyone and ending up in prison." Tod rudely blurted on our ride home. I vividly remember how hot my body became in an instant. I wanted so badly to just stick him in his jaw with my fist while he drove. Instead, I opened the passenger door to his suburban while he was driving and told him to stop and let me off. He stopped his vehicle, and with only being a few blocks from the house, he allowed me to walk the rest of the way home. Once I walked in, Kimberly kindly asked if I could do the dishes. Though I was still hot from what Tod had said, I did what she asked to shut them both up and get off my case.

"Brandy, I understand you are upset." Kimberly gently approached me and began to speak. "But you know you're not allowed to see or speak with your family. It's not our rules, it's the agency's rules. If you stop breaking them, then you won't be getting in trouble as much." She gently reminded me. "Kim, leave me alone please." I told her as I tried my best to control my raging anger. She wasn't trying to be mean, but I was beyond frustrated and annoyed in that moment.

"Get away from her Kimberly, she might hit you." Tod came in and interrupted. Kim took a few steps back and they both stared at me from across the kitchen as if I were an animal at the zoo that they didn't want to get near. I looked at Tod, "You don't know my mom to be talking about her like that." I told him bitterly, trying not to allow the tears that were glossed over my eyes run.

"Well, I know enough to know she didn't care enough to change for y'all. That's why she's in prison now." He said with pride. It was like he had been trying to get under my skin so I could pop off.

"SHUT UP TOD!" I yelled at the top of my lungs and threw the silverware that I had in my hands on the floor, then ran for my room. I cried myself to sleep that night, hating my life. The day came where I truly began to miss my mom. Yes, the memories of her heavy drug use would haunt me. But the memories of her kissing my forehead randomly, her joyful laugh, her sweet smile, watching The Wizard of Oz or Mary Poppins with me, or her kissing my cheek before getting on the bus began to trump the bad memories. Again, before the drugs, I remembered my mom. Remembered that she was once a sound minded, sweet hearted woman who loved me. I slowly began to choose to remember that mom instead of the one I knew deep down she wasn't. The one that drugs drove her to become. I would lay in my bed at night, staring out of my window looking at the moon. Wondering if wherever my mom was, if she was looking at it too.

I began to think about how she was raised. She never knew her dad either. He left her when she was young too. She, my two aunts and uncle grew up in a toxic environment of drug use and abuse. She moved in with my dad at age fifteen, and had me at eighteen. Which made me wonder if anyone ever took time to show her a better path.

Her empty voids and hurts had led her to make self harming choices. I began to understand. Empathy ran over my body for my sweet mom. She didn't have it so easy herself. Realization after realization hit. She was the oldest of four siblings, so I could imagine and relate to the responsibility. Tears ran down the sides of my eyes as I laid there and just missed her terribly. *I miss you mom. I forgive you,* I said in my heart one night.

The day after, I was determined to find out which prison she was in, and how I could write her. A family member I secretly got a hold of gave me her address, and I asked one of my best friends at the time, if I could write her from her address. Her parents knew about my situation and freely opened their home to where I could use their house and address to write to her. I could see the compassion my friend's mom had for me, putting herself in my mother's shoes. How hard would it be to be defined as a recovering addict, finally sober, and not knowing how your children are? Maybe regretting everything you put them through but having cuffs around your hands, literally. Only praying that they still loved you, and maybe just maybe find it in their hearts to forgive you. I'll always appreciate my friends' family. For about two months, my mom and I wrote to each other back and forth. The first letter was the deepest of course. I told her how I was at first so angry with her, and how I felt as if I could go the rest of my life without seeing her. But how I somehow found it in me to love her again and forgive her. When she first wrote back, I was so excited. She told me how she had been praying for me and my sisters to forgive her. In future letters she would talk about how she'd changed, gave her life to God and when she was released how she promised she would get us back. How our new case investigator would go to visit her and tell her to sign her rights away and just let us be adopted, because she didn't have a chance with us anymore. That she messed up too bad. Nevertheless, she refused. She would tell me that God told her she would get her girls back.

I didn't know God, and my mom had lied more times than I could count before, so I couldn't depend on that word. But I deeply wanted to believe it would someday happen and give her the benefit of the doubt.

CHAPTER

Eleven

One careless day, I had a letter ready to send to my mom in my gym bag, which I would take to school of course. Until this day, I have no idea how it escaped from my bag and ended up in my investigator's hands. My fifth period classroom intercom came on.

"Could we please have Brandy Tijerina come to the office." It blared into the classroom. At that point, I had yet to know my letter was gone. Me being called to the principal's office struck me with curiosity. I entered the principal's office, and there sat my least favorite person, next to Tod, my investigator. *What is she doing here?* I thought. She got up to close the door behind me with a threatening look in her eyes. Tod didn't stay and I noticed no one else was in the office.

"SIT." She commanded. I found a seat and sat. She always scared me a little bit. She was tall, heavier set, had short black hair, braces, yet always dressed up very nicely. But somehow, just like with Tod, I didn't trust her. When she would check on us during home visits, she mainly just listened to what Tod had to say. Never really bothered to truly listen to me or allow me to express my concerns. "So, little Ms. Brandy. How's your mom doing these days?" She sneered at me. I was in shock. Why would she ask that question?

"Uhm... I don't know. Why?" Not knowing what else to say. Without beating around any bush, she pulled a white envelope from her oversized light brown Coach purse. WHAM! She slammed it on the principal's desk.

"Well you should know if you're writing to her in prison!" Her voice began to raise a pitch.

"Okay. So what? She's my mom and I miss her. You can't keep me from writing to her." I said with an attitude while rolling my eyes.

"Oh! You wanna catch an attitude with me little girl? Act like a witch, and I'll treat you like a witch! And what I mean by that is if you want to continue writing to your mother, then I will send you so far away where you won't even be able to think about her, do you understand me?!" She roared. I was floored. A knot filled my throat, but I dared not show her my feelings.

"Fine, are we done yet?" I responded with a monotone voice.

"We're done when I say we're done Brandy!" Do you know how hard Tod and Kimberly are working to adopt you three? But you writing your mother giving her hope that she'll be able to get y'all back will get in the way." She continued her rant at me. I snapped back "I don't want to be adopted! And neither do my sisters. They miss my mom too and want to go back with her when she gets out."

"Well that's too bad little girl, because the judge won't let your mom have y'all back. She's too unstable and won't be able to prove that she can stay off of drugs." She snorted at me.

"You don't know that!" I yelled!

"You poor little girl... you'll see. Now do I make myself clear about writing to her?" She said, a note of finality in her voice.

"Crystal." I glared. She opened the door and replied to me with a snarky "have a great rest of your day."

I had no response, and just walked past her and went back to class with a heavy heart. The rest of the day was cloudy mentally. I couldn't focus during track practice; I told my coach I wasn't feeling well and sat out for the day. How did that letter get to her? Did Tod somehow go through my bag before school started? When I got home, nothing new, I was grounded for the rest of the school year. About a month left, oh well. The only thing that upset me about being grounded was that I wouldn't be able to see the guy I would mess around with. The Senior who made me feel wanted but only used me. I had ended up finding out he had a girlfriend earlier in the year. However, I grew use to being with guys who had a girlfriend, so

I didn't care much anymore. I finally accepted that I was no longer worthy enough to be first. Only seconds. With him, he had respect in school and on the streets with older people. I learned how he had so much money by being at his house and seeing his hustle. His money never really phased me. I just felt protected with him.

People actually began to know me as one of the dealer's girls. It was always between me and his original girlfriend that people would get us confused with. One day I'd be at a party with him, the next it was her. She and I both knew of each other. We even fist fought over him one night. It didn't change anything though, we both wanted his affection, wouldn't give him up and that only made him proud. Two vulnerable girls thirsting for love in all the wrong places. So yes, he was the only thing I was worried about losing if I didn't see him for too long. There was only one thing for me to start doing again, sneaking out to see him. I told him at school when to be down the street from my house. At that time every other night, he'd meet me in the spot. I became such a pro at it, that I thankfully was never caught.

Summer came, once again. I was ungrounded and the summer began just as I planned. Always (supposedly) staying at different friends' houses but staying at my main guy's house. It wasn't too far into the summer of 2008. My guy had just graduated, and parties were still going on every other day since the last day of school. I woke up with a slight hangover, makeup lingering on my face from the night before. I was out of clothes and needed to go home for the first time in three days to restock. My guy parked down the street, planning to be there again in two hours so he could drop me off at the town carnival that evening. As I made my way to the house, I began to notice multiple cars parked in front of Tod and Kim's. The closer I got, the more I realized it was my investigators car, my caseworker's car, and my CASA worker's car. I thought it was an odd sight because my visit from them wasn't due for another few weeks or so. I nervously walked through the front door, and saw my enemy standing what it felt like seven feet tall, staring a hole through me.

"Hi Brandy, we've been expecting you. Come and sit." My investigator said with a smirk running across her mouth. I walked into the front living room with so many faces staring at me.

"I want to show you something." She pulled out a letter that my mom had sent me. It was a letter that I had hidden in my room. *How did they find it?* I guess they searched for proof that I was still messing up, and there it was.

"I warned you Brandy. Go pack your bags, you're coming with us." She snapped.

"W... what? Where am I going?" I answered hesitantly.

"You'll find out when you get there. Since you took forever to get home, you now have fifteen minutes to pack. If I were you, I'd hurry up." She replied. I couldn't believe what I was hearing. I looked at Tod and Kimberly in confusion; they looked away.

"Where are my sisters?" I asked them.

"They'll come and say bye when you're done packing. Now go. You're at thirteen minutes." She answered in a haughty tone. I felt so much rage boil up in me. I could run out of the front door right then, but what would I do from there? Defeated, I headed for my room to pack. But first, I needed to call my guy. I needed to let him know what was going on. Maybe he'd come get me from wherever I was going. Even though I knew I wasn't his top priority, I knew he at least cared. And when he told me he loved me, I wanted to believe it. So maybe just maybe he would consider it.

"Phone, please." Margi, my CASA worker had followed me in my room, ninja style. A little startled, my heart dropped. "I can't keep my phone?" I said with sorrow.

"I'm sorry, Brandy. If it was up to me." She gave me a look of empathy. I said no more and gave her my phone. I had respect for her. The times she'd come to visit us, she sat, and she listened. Never judged me, never preached to me. Just listened.

The way she wouldn't rush me and gave me her full attention gave me confidence to trust her. Not enough to spill all of the beans that I was doing behind closed doors; I was always ashamed of that. Just enough to express a little of what I could articulate, as far as what was going on inside of me.

"Pack what you can. If you need anything else, The Children's Home will provide it." She said gently.

"The Children's Home?!" I said with so much hurt in my heart. The times that Tod and Kimberly would take us there to get clothes, I always felt sorry for the kids there. I never wanted to live there. In my young mind, it seemed like a children's prison and there I was getting sent there.

"I'm sorry Brandy, the Thompsons had no other choice. Maybe it won't be for long, if you can prove that you really are a sweet girl. The sweet girl I see." She gently told me.

Hot tears began to fall from my eyes as I packed. I had no more words; it was happening. Ten minutes flew by.

"KNOCK KNOCK, times up Miss. Brandy. Let's get you going." My investigator ushered me along. I couldn't even look at her. I could not stand that woman. I walked out into the hallway and made my way to the front door.

"Girls!" Tod shouted. Alexis and Jasmine slowly came in from the back din and walked to where I was standing. "Say bye to your sister. She's going to The Children's Home for a little while."

"Will she be back?" Alexis asked, confused.

"We hope so." Tod looked at me with insincere eyes. I knelt down and hugged my sisters, quietly sobbing. I had failed them, just like my mom did. I was so ashamed. I didn't trust Tod from the get-go, there was always just something about him that never sat well with me, yet I left my sisters in his hands each time I chose my friends and boys over them. Only in hopes that my gut about him was wrong but now, I wouldn't be around even if I wanted to be.

"I love y'all, okay? I'm so sorry Lex." I looked Alexis in her eyes, knowing she was old enough to remember how it was with mom, and now what was happening. "It won't be long until we're together again." I gave them one last long hug, wiped my tears, and stood with my head high.

"Okay, I'm ready." I said.

Thankfully it was Kelsey, my caseworker's duty to drive me, and not my investigator. Kelsey became our caseworker a few months after Nicole. She was pretty cool.

I mean I didn't dislike her. She was nice and would talk about her personal life as if she trusted me.

Nothing too deep, but basics about her daughter and such. It didn't bother me. It was nice to hear about normal lives; but oh, was that drive to Lubbock a gloomy one. She didn't have much to say at all that day. Only an hour away but seemed like a whole day.

"Kelsey..." I spoke from the back seat. "Can I please make a call? Please. It's my best friend." I asked with hopeful eyes. She looked back at me using her rear- view mirror. She sighed, "Five minutes." She handed me her cell phone. I dialed my guys number in hopes he would answer and not be with his other girlfriend.

"Hello", his voice fell out of the phone.

"Bobby... they took me." I began to tear up. Saying it out loud hit differently.

"What? Who took you? Where?" He replied with concern in his voice.

"CPS. I'm on my way to The Children's Home. I just wanted to call and let you know." I told him with a quiver in my voice. To my surprise, he actually sounded concerned. "Brandy, stop lying."

"I'm serious! I don't have time to explain. And I don't know when I'll be able to talk to you again. I just wanted you to know I love you." I stated. There was a brief silence.

"I love you too, Brandy. Call me as soon as you can okay?" He responded with sincerity.

It was as if his whole macho man demeanor vanished and actual care began to come from his heart. I heard it in his voice that he became sad. It was just what I needed at that moment. To be wanted and to know I mattered. A feeling that for some reason, only boys could make me feel.

"I will." I replied. Kelsey lifted her hand toward the back seat.

"I've gotta go. I'll call you soon." I said, preparing to hand the phone back.

"No Brandy wait..." Bobby pleaded.

"Bobby, I have to go. I love you. Bye." I hung up to respect the chance that Kelsey gave me. *It's going to be okay, girl.* I leaned my head against the window the rest of the way, watching the mild rain fall on that cloudy day.

When we arrived at The Children's Home around nine pm, the first thing I thought was how it was in the middle of nowhere. Not a chance to run away and make it. When we walked into the emergency shelter, it was already lights out. Quiet and still.

"Hi... I'm Ms. Donna" A tall white lady with short light brown hair approached me and kindly whispered.

Kelsey leaned towards my ear and began to whisper too. "This is the director here, she's gonna show you your room while I do some paperwork. I'll come and check on you in a few days okay?" I looked at her like that's it? "You're leaving?" I asked.

"After the paperwork, yes. Ms. Donna is gonna show you your room." She repeated. "Get some rest,

I know it's been a long day for you." I looked at Ms. Donna motioning for me to follow her. I picked up my small black gym bag of clothes and followed. She led me down a hall to the right side of the small living area. A hall that had a sign that read "Girls Hall" before entering. She made a right into the first room I saw. There were two twin sized beds and a small wooden nightstand in the center of them. One bed on the left, and one on the right. The bed on the right was already occupied with a girl who was sleeping. Ms. Donna stood next to the left bed and patted it, signing that it was mine. The top layer was like a green plastic material. At the end of the bed was a bed sheet, a white quilt like blanket, and a pillow.

"Just leave your bag right there and we'll wash your clothes tomorrow. Go ahead and get some sleep and we'll explain everything in the morning. The bathroom is right across the hallway if you need it. Are you okay?" She whispered.

"Yeah." I said. Yet felt everything but okay.

"Okay. Goodnight Brandy." She smiled and walked out leaving the door open. I stood there for a good minute looking at my bed. Wondering how in the world this was my life. I felt so defeated and like such a lame failure. Finally, I crawled onto the plastic-coated mattress without putting the sheet on, grabbed the blanket at my feet, covered my head, and cried myself to sleep.

DING DING DING DING! My body shot up to the sound of a little metal bell. I looked around forgetting where I was. Wishing it was all a bad dream.

"Okay girls, up up up! Make those beds and brush y'all's teeth! Breakfast will be served in fifteen minutes!" A woman's joyful yet bold voice projected in from the hallway.

"Hey? When did you get here?" A white girl with pink boy cut hair stretched, yawned and asked with ease.

"Last night. You were sleeping." I replied.

"Oh no, was I snoring? My last roommate said I snore." She asked me, with doubt in her voice.

I smiled. "Nah, you're good." My eyes felt puffy and my head still hurt from crying all night. I was so tired. I felt as if I had no sleep at all. The girl noticed my demeanor.

"Is it your first time here?" She asked me as she started making her bed, so I did the same.

"Yeah. Yours?" I answered.

"Neh. I was here before I almost got adopted. My foster parents didn't go through with it, so they sent me back here. Oh well though. I'm already seventeen. I'm getting ready to emancipate myself and live on my own. Only a few more months, if I can keep my mouth shut. But Ms. Lucy be testing me. How old are you?" She said, the words spilling out of her mouth.

"Sixteen." I replied. "What does emancipate mean? Can I do that?".

"It means you can basically sign yourself out of foster care if you can prove that you are capable of taking care of yourself and stay out of trouble. But first, you've gotta be seventeen." She told me, with a matter of fact attitude. I hung my head at the thought of me having almost a whole year until I was seventeen. It was only the beginning of June and I had just turned sixteen at the end of March.

"What's your name?" She asked me. "Brandy." I replied.

"Well Brandy, how this works is when they wake us up, make your bed as fast as possible so you can have a little longer in the bathroom to pee and brush your teeth. Then we head to the kitchen table to have some grub. Then we all take turns showering. We have about ten solid minutes each. Make sure you're not longer than fifteen minutes total in there or Ms. Lucy will start being annoying. After we shower, we hang out in the living room to wait on everyone to shower and get dressed. Then staff comes and lets us know what we have going for the day. Sometimes they take us to the lake. If not, there's a pool here, a gym where we can shoot some hoops and stuff. Then there's the park. Anyway, I'm gonna go brush my teeth. I'll see you at the table." She explained quickly to me.

"Everything okay? Did Mitsy explain how the morning routine works?" A staff member popped

her head through our open room door with a smile. I assumed it was the Ms. Lucy Mitsy was referring to. Although her vibe didn't seem annoying.

"Yeah. Just gotta brush my teeth." I replied.

"Alright. See you at the table in fifteen." She calmly said as she walked away. I wondered what time it was. It had to have been around eight in the morning. I hated that thought. It was summertime for crying out loud. I was usually up by noon, then I could get my day started. This was madness. After introducing myself to the few girls who asked on my way to the bathroom, I did my business and followed another girl to the dining room table. I quickly glanced around the place, noticing a chart of colors on a wall in the dining area with names on each color. Purple read good behavior, blue read warning, orange read chaperoned, and red read lock down. I wondered what that was about. They served us cereal, and toast with a cup of both orange juice and milk.

"Are we not having grape jelly today?" My roommate asked with a disappointed tone in her voice.

"No ma'am, just strawberry." Ms. Lucy replied. "Well that's dumb." She rolled her eyes. I seen Ms. Lucy brush the comment off as she seemed used to push back.

I sat and looked around the table. There were maybe twelve of us total. Half girls, half boys. Most of them looked younger than me, between the ages of about eight through seventeen, all blend of races. I wondered if I was one of the oldest. There was small chit chatter going on all around me between them all.

I kept my head down while I played with my cereal a bit. I didn't want to look up and allow them to see my glossy eyes and lips quiver from the knot that was burning in my throat. I still couldn't believe I was there. I already missed my freedom and despised the fact that we had a schedule to go by. All my life I had no order and barely any rules. Even at my moms, considering I was mostly the "adult". Then coming to a place where there was nothing but order and rules. I was juked. Once we were all done with breakfast time, it was then time to get dressed for the day and meet in the living area. I went to my room to pick out what I should wear for this miserable day.

"Pick an outfit, then you can fold and put the rest of your clothes in that cabinet right there. When you're done, meet us in the living area", said Ms. Hollyn, another staff member who came in behind me, pointing to a white cabinet on the right-side wall of the room, at the end of Mitsy's bed.

"Do I get to shower?" I asked.

"You can either shower before bed or before breakfast. Today it looks like you chose to shower before bed." She saw my demeanor become a little frustrated. "Don't worry girly, you'll get this schedule down in no time." Optimism reigned through her jolly voice. She seemed so peppy.

"Ten minutes girls!" She announced in the hallway, headed back to the living area. I quickly chose the outfit, changed, and did as she said. I was one of the last ones to enter the living area and simply chose a seat.

"Oh, Michael usually sits there. He's at a visit with his mom, he'll be back later. You can sit right here if you want? It's not assigned to anyone or anything." A friendly smile came from a little brown eyed beauty.

"Thanks", I said next to her. Kids continued to chatter as we all waited for staff to come and let us know what the plan was for the day.

"What's your name?" I asked.

"Aubri" She smiled brightly, "what's yours?". "Brandy." I smiled back.

"It gets easier. I saw your face at breakfast. I know that feeling. But yeah, it's not so bad here." She said confidently.

"How long have you been here?" I asked her.

"In the Mason? For about two months. Here at The Children's Home for four years. I'm hoping to be adopted next month. That's why they have me here at the Mason. There's this family that wants me. I've been able to have weekend visits with them, and I think I like them. So, I hope they go through with it." She said with hope.

"Wow... adopted huh? You don't wanna go back with your mom?" I asked in wonder.

"I did... until she signed her rights away two years ago." Aubri replied. My heart dropped. She saw the look on my face.

"It's okay." She giggled. "I'm better now. I just really hope this family actually adopts me. Then I'll really feel better. I'll be able to see my brother more often since this family said they wouldn't mind."

"Your brother? Where is he?" I asked her.

"He was adopted last year. The family that adopted him didn't want a teenager, so they had to split us. He was six." What did she mean by feeling better? How could her mom just give up on her? She seemed so sweet. My heart ached for her in that moment.

"I can't believe you've been here for four years. I feel like I'm gonna go crazy and I haven't even been here a day." I told her. Aubri laughed. "Why did you get put into foster care?" She so plainly asked, to continue the conversation.

To my surprise, I couldn't remember the last time someone asked me. Out in the free world, if someone had asked, I would crouch and feel embarrassment. All of my friends from school had what seemed to be decent lives. Brick and clean homes, nice clothes, their parents cared for and wanted them. Thankfully, even though they lived blessed lives, they never saw me any different from them. They saw me for me but even so on the inside, I never felt like I belonged and could never measure up. But with Aubri, at that moment, I belonged.

"My mom was bad on drugs. It got the best of her when I was younger and now, I'm here." I said quickly.

"Man, I hate drugs. That's why a lot of kids are here." She said with passion.

"Is that what happened to you too?" I asked her.

"No. A family member... he...." Her head hung. My body ran cold for a quick second. I understood without her having to go any further. A quick flash of what the family friend did to me made me cringe.

"I'm so sorry Aubri..." I placed my hand on her shoulder. She looked up at me and smiled. "It's okay. Like I said before, it gets better." Her strength amazed me.

"Okay ladies and gents! Today is teen day! If you are thirteen and up, and would like to participate in teen night, come on over to sign the clipboard. I'll be back to pick y'all up at five thirty!" A tall, thin white friendly looking man with brunette hair came in the front door and stole our attention. I looked at Aubri in confusion. "What's teen day?".

"Once a week, they take just us teens to either a park in town, or the movies. Only if you're on purple of course." She explained to me. At once, there it was: my grand epiphany. One of my first thoughts of being there was how I could run away. But I knew I wouldn't succeed since we were so far out.

"Aubri... can you keep a secret?" I whispered to her. "Yeah, of course." She leaned in.

"I want to run. Do you think I could run if I went to teen night?" I asked, my voice barely a sigh. Her eyes popped out at me. "Honestly, if they take us to the movies, you might have a chance. But if they take us to the park, you won't make it. Trust me, I tried after my brother was adopted, but they caught me. Then I was on red for a month. No freedom." She explained to me.

"Okay, well how do we know where they're gonna take us?" I asked.

"You find out once you get in the van." She got up to go put her name on the clipboard. I rose and went to find staff.

"Ms. Hollyn, can I go to teen night?" I asked.

"Course' you can, Sweets! Just go sign the clipboard." Replied Ms. Hollyn. I walked over to get in the small line of about four teens.

"Is that all the teens that go?" I asked Aubri as we both went back to the living area.

"Nah. If cottage eight and nine are on good behavior, then they'll come too."

"Cottage eight and nine?" I asked curiously.

"Yeah, we're in the Mason, the emergency shelter. The cottages are where kids actually live. Like forever unless they're adopted." She explained to me. I was so thankful for Aubri. She was so nice and just so patient with teaching me about how that place was ran. The more she told me, the more I became anxious to go to teen night to make my move. The morning flew by with playing basketball in the gym, within the Children's Home area. But once lunch and chore time were over, the announcement was made.

"Alright teens, Mr. Brian is about to be here to pick y'all up. Whoever signed up for teen night, be ready in five minutes." Ms. Lucy announced. I had to think quickly. I obviously couldn't take my clothes with me, so I slipped off to my room and contemplated on what to take. I was wearing my Brownfield Cubs red t-shirt, and blue jean stretchy capris. I thought it was perfect. But looking down at my feet, I realized I wouldn't get very far with sandals on. So, I pulled out my one pair of red and white Nike Shox that I borrowed from my best friend Kory, and never returned. Laced them up and felt confident that the outfit would do for running. I looked around and wondered if I should take anything. There was only one thing I dared not leave, and that was my Chi hair straightener that I stole. Tucked it in my fake Coach purse, and that was it. I was ready.

"Teens, van is here!" Rang out through the halls. My heart skipped a beat. I walked back through the hallway towards the front door. Aubri seemed to be waiting on me. We walked out together, and each hopped into the huge white van, joining the other teens from the cottages. I didn't want to do the whole small talk thing. I just wanted to sit quiet in the back of the van with Aubri and wait for the word on where they decided to take us. Fingers crossed that the movies were the plan. Christian music was softly playing in the background

while all the teens caught up. Tod and Kimberly were always playing Christian music in the Suburban, and I always got annoyed by it. Which is what I felt in that van. I wanted so bad just to be in my room listening to my music, alone. I was tired of meeting new people.

"You okay?" Aubri asked.

"Yeah, I'm just ready for them to say where we're going." I responded. She had no response. Upon entering the small city by crossing the Lubbock population sign, the staff member that was driving turned the radio all the way down.

"Alright y'all, so tonight is movie night." He announced.

"Yes." We heard a few teens say at the same time under their breath. Meanwhile, Aubri and I locked eyes, knowing what was ahead at that point.

"What are we watching?" A teen asked.

"Chronicles of Narnia...the new one." Staff responded.

"Man, that movie's wack. We should watch Eagle Eye." A teen boy blurted.

"Sorry, it wasn't up to me, Bud. Besides, I heard it was really good. You never know, you might like it." The staff member said in a chipper tone. While they were talking about the movie, I was still in semi shock that this teen night fell in my favor. I had to think of a plan.

CHAPTER

Twelve

After arriving at the theater and getting the whole snack bar shenanigans situated, we each snuggled into seats that were beneath the few staff. There must have been about fourteen of us total. If it were just us four from the Mason, it would have been a high risk to go forth with what I had planned once the movie was rolling. The previews took forever and a day to play, but I was glad. It gave me time to truly decide what I was about to do. Half of me was trying to convince myself not to do it. Not to run. To just suck it up, behave as best I could and maybe get sent back to

Tod and Kimberly's soon. But the other half knew how much Tod wanted to get rid of me. So, no telling if he'd ever want me back in his home or not. Almost every adult that was ever in my life had lied to me. *Why should I have taken his word?* The movie began. Although my eyes were fixed on the screen, I paid no attention to what was going on mentally. Solely thinking of my next move. I waited about twenty minutes, then finally bit the bullet and decided. My decision which brings us full circle. I did it, I ran.

Once gathering myself at that dingy brown dumpster in that random alley, I got back to running. My first thought was to find a pay phone. I needed to call my guy. I had a deep feeling he would come get me if I did. At least I hoped. Thankfully, a laundry mat came to sight not too long after leaving the dumpster. I instantly noticed the payphone by itself right outside the place. I ran up to it, looked over both shoulders before dialing. Still so paranoid that I was about to get caught. Once I saw the coast was still clear, I dialed the number I knew by heart; but what do you know, no dial tone. I pulled the return change lever, but it refused to give me back my fifty cents. The only thing I had on me other than my fake Coach purse and hair straightener. I had to think fast. I glanced to the left under a bridge, across the highway and noticed a Texas Land and Cattle restaurant on the corner of a busy street and went for it. Upon approaching the parking lot, I noticed that there were lots of cars there. I remembered how sweaty I felt. And could only imagine how my face looked with all the crying I had done. So, I went for the next place, Long John Silvers. Which had very few cars. Much better for myself. Gasping for air, I barged into the small fast food restaurant.

"Hi, can I please borrow a phone? My car broke down outside and I just really need to call for help." Tears were flowing down my face uncontrollably. The worker looked at me with concern in his eyes. "Sh... sure." He unintentionally hesitated, handing me the wireless store phone. "Here's a cup for a fountain drink too." He offered. I gladly accepted. I was burning up and past thirsty. I dialed the phone. "Hello." A voice said.

"Hey! I ran! Can you come get me?!" I said quickly. "Wait... what! Brandy? Is that you?" Bobby said.

"Yes! Can you please come get me? I'm at a Long John Silver's off of the loop here in Lubbock. Please!" I begged desperately.

"Brandy, you can't run. You're gonna get in more trouble. You have to go back." He said with disbelief in his voice.

"I'm not going back. I'm not. If you can't come get me, I'll find someone who will!" I began to tear up. Trying to hurry up the conversation, scared that I'd see a white van outside any minute.

"Wait. Okay, okay... I'm actually here in Lubbock on my way to the Bun B concert. I'm about five minutes

away from that Long John Silvers. I'll be there." He promised me.

I couldn't believe my ears. I honestly thought I was going to have to wait for at least forty-five minutes for him to drive to where I was. By some amazing act, he was right down the road from me.

Within minutes, I spotted him from inside the restaurant as he drove up in a white, two door Honda, with an older friend that I didn't recognize. I briefly thanked the workers for the phone without making eye contact, ran to and pushed the Long Johns door open and within steps, practically fell into his arms as he stepped out of the car. I was never so happy to see him. I cried in his chest for a quick second feeling such relief before I snapped out of it and climbed in the back seat before I was seen by anyone else. His friend who was driving sped off onto the Lubbock freeway.

"Brandy, what were you thinking?" He asked in a concerned manner.

"I told you... I couldn't stay there. There was no way I would be able to talk to you, there was no freedom, everything was a schedule and... I just couldn't stay there!" I began to become frustrated.

I needed him to just understand and stop asking questions. My mind was still racing, and my heart was still pounding. I wondered what the staff was saying or even thinking at this point. Would they really look for me? Or would they just let me be?

CHAPTER

Thirteen

It had been about eleven months of being on the run. April 18th, 2009 was the day I gave up mentally. I had been through the rut. I had just turned seventeen close to a month prior. I sat high as a kite thinking about how I would call my caseworker to tell her I was throwing up my white flag. I had town hopped for nearly a whole year. Throughout the year, I would make any place work for shelter. All over Texas I went staying with different people. Friends of friends, distant family, strangers etc. From Lubbock to Midland, to Junction, to Waco, to Bryan and a fewsmall towns. I was homeless, almost got choked to death by a man at one point, became a heavy smoker of pot, battled depression, sold weed for a dealer, was a thief, a great liar, more promiscuous than I had ever been and had no hope for a future. I was always only thinking about my next meal, and if I'd have a place to stay. All of that baggage including the heaviest; fear of being caught. I hated foster care and didn't wanna go back.

However, I had come to the realization that I was indeed exhausted. I missed my sisters, school, my friends, and the simple things such as walking in a store without feeling like I was going to get caught. In that season I wasn't too far from home. I was within two hours from Lubbock and began to ponder on how I was going to make the move of turning myself in. Something I had kept in my one little purse that journeyed along with me was my caseworkers phone number. In the beginning of the journey, I never thought I'd need it again, but for some reason, I couldn't come to a peace about throwing it away. And when time came of wanting to turn myself in, I was glad I didn't. April 20th was just two days away. And what that day is, is where every pot smoker across the nation smokes pot all day to celebrate the drug, in a sense. Me being a heavy smoker, I decided that I would enjoy my last bit of freedom by celebrating 4/20, then I would do it. I would make the call to my caseworker. Which is exactly what did. I made my way back to Brownfield where I stayed with a friend for the night while partaking in the pothead holiday. The next day, April twenty first I made the call.

"Kelsey, it's Brandy." I said bluntly.

"Oh my goodness, Brandy! How are you? Are you okay? Where are you?" I heard the concern in her voice as she bombarded me with questions that I was not up for answering at that moment.

"I'm fine... I'm done. I'm turning myself in." There was a brief pause. "What do I need to do, Kelsey?" I broke the thin ice.

"Okay... okay..." She sounded a little frantic. "C... can I pick you up tomorrow somewhere?" I could tell she was in disbelief.

"Uh, sure." I answered without even thinking about it.

"Okay, you name the place and I'll be there." She told me quickly. I had to think for a split second. I was only forty-five minutes away from Lubbock, and I knew my friend wouldn't mind driving me there if I asked.

"How about the McDonalds in front of the mall in Lubbock?" I suggested.

"Perfect!" She exclaimed. "I'll be there. Shall we say 2pm?".

"Uhmm, how about like 7pm-ish." I replied. I wanted to have a full day out so that when I got back to the children's home it would be lights out and I wouldn't cause a scene.

"O... kay." She hesitated. "Sure, I can do that." She confirmed.

"Well alright, I guess I'll see you then." I began to conclude the brief conversation.

"Alright, sounds great!" There was another minor pause. "Brandy, I'm really glad you called. And I'm so happy to know you're okay. Please know that I am so proud of your decision. Things will get better from here, okay? Please don't bail on me tomorrow." A knot filled my throat. *Everything will be okay? What did that even mean?* Ignoring my feelings, I promised I wouldn't bail, confirmed that my mind was made up and that I'd be there. Before I knew it, the next day came and flew. Six pm had crept and I began to second guess myself. I was nervous. *What was to happen once I got to the children's home? Was the hateful investigator still assigned to my case?* I hoped not. She was the last person I wanted to see. I just hoped that what my roommate had said almost a year ago was true. That if I could prove I was responsible enough to take care of myself, I would be approved for emancipation. I only hoped. But despite my hope or feelings, I knew in my gut that I was doing the right thing.

My friend kindly drove me to Lubbock and dropped me off where me and Kelsey agreed to meet. I was about twenty minutes early because I didn't want her seeing who drove me. There I sat at an empty booth; with my one bag of a few outfits I had accumulated throughout the year. I stared outside of the window

With my mind and heart numb. Moments later, I recognized a red SUV pulling up right in front of the window I was staring out of. Sure enough, it was my caseworker. We both locked eyes through the window and smiled at the same time. I wasn't sure what I was feeling in that moment, but I now know it was hope. Hope is what I felt. I grabbed my bag, made my way to her car and hopped in her passenger seat.

"Well hi there." She said with gladness in her voice, smiling from ear to ear.

"Hi." I giggled.

"You look great Brandy." She told me with a smile. "Yeah right, I've gained like a million pounds." I

said back to her.

"Oh goodness, don't start with that again." She laughed. I used to vent to her about my body image issues and she was always trying to affirm me in that area.

"Well, you ready?" She asked optimistically. I took a deep breath. "Yep. I guess so."

It was about a twenty-minute drive out to the children's home, just enough time for small talk.

"You know, you are one tough cookie, girl. I worried about you so much. There were times where I just knew we would find you, but then you'd slip right through our fingers." She began.

"Kelsey, don't you know I'm always one step ahead?" I joked.

"I know that's right. You proved me wrong. How in the world did you survive? You were sixteen Brandy." She emphasized. I had a moment of flashbacks. Buses, escaping, sleeping in abandoned houses, strangers, random hook ups, partying, and abuse.

"It was a long year." Is all I had energy to say. We made it to the children's home and still, my mind and heart were numb. The first time going there to live, I was full of anxiety, fear and anger. This time, I just let it be. I was tired.

"You okay?" Kelsey asked.

"Yes. Let's get this over with." I said, looking out to the building. I opened the car door and began walking toward the Mason Cottage. The sun was setting so I knew it was just about time for lights out. School was still in session, so I was glad to have gotten there later in the day to not contact anyone. I just wanted to sleep. I sat in the living area while Kelsey took care of some paperwork. Approaching nine pm, she assured me that she would come check on me the following day and made her exit. Night staff directed me to my room. The very same room I was in a year prior. Even the very same bed. Only this time, there was a different roommate snoring in there. I could tell by her long black hair. I plopped my body on the twin sized bed and the smell of clean sheets brought me a sense of peace. There in that moment, I soaked in the reality of being safe and no longer running. Yet, as tired as I was, I still couldn't fall asleep. I tossed and turned for about an hour before I gave up and just opened my eyes to stare at the ceiling. It was dark, but the moonlight was shining brightly and directly into the room.

There I laid with so many thoughts wandering around in my head. I couldn't gain control of them. The voice of my dad saying *I'll be back mija, I promise.* The paralyzing fear that took over my body when the family friend took my innocence at age six, and all of the others. The long days and nights of taking care of my sisters and crying myself to sleep wishing I had a different life, like the kids at school. All of the times I tried to be enough for guys by giving my body away. Trying to prove that I am beautiful, and worthy of being more than just a hookup or side piece, but never succeeded. The haunting memory of the man's hands around my neck, squeezing the life out of me until I nearly died.

There was screaming in my soul; I just wanted to be free. I wanted the pain to stop already. Tears began to roll nonstop down the sides of my face. Wailing inside, but I dared not make a sound. All I could do was open my mouth to release the cry, but again… not make a sound. I realized that my soul was in agony. I, Eloisa Brandy Tijerina, was at my wits-end. When suddenly, at the very back of the haunting memories, I began to hear a melody that I learned in vacation bible school back when my mom would pawn me off to church for the day.

"Jesus loves me this I know, for the Bible tells me so. Little ones to Him belong, they are weak, but He is strong. Yes, Jesus loves me…" My heart began to pound; my palms began to sweat. Why was this song all of a sudden blaring in my head? And what was this insane feeling coming over me?

Then, without even thinking, I rose to my feet and faced the window where the blinds were open, and the moon struck me with peace. It was as if someone else was in that room leading my every move. I barely realized that I suddenly didn't feel alone inside. And as I stared at the moon, my mouth opened, and I began to whisper words from the depth of my heart.

"Jesus. If you're really real the way people have said you are all my life, please help me. I don't want to live like this anymore. I don't want to hurt. There has got to be more to life than this. I'm tired. I'm just tired." My head drooped in surrender, I collapsed to my knees and bawled. By a miracle my roommate didn't wake up. There I was in the middle of that room, April 22nd, 2009 surrendering to a God that I never knew could or would come into my life and wreck me in the best of ways. I sobbed and sobbed until I had no tears left. I crawled back into my bed and fell fast asleep.

Chapter

Fourteen

The next morning, I woke up to cherry blossom body spray lingering in the room.

"Hey..." My roommate said while putting deodorant on, nearly hovering over me.

"Hey..." I responded, looking up at her, trying to open my eyes.

"How old are you?" She bluntly asked. "Seventeen." I replied.

"Dang, so you're like a junior huh." She said.

"Nah, I'm not in school." I explained. "Oh, for real?" She said with curiosity. "Yeah, I just turned myself in last night."

"Oh dang, you ran?" I heard excitement in her voice.

"Yeah, last year. But trust me, I wouldn't recommend it." I told her, honestly.

"Girls, five minutes!" We heard staff calling. "Well, you gonna be here after school?" She asked. "Yeah I think so." I replied.

"Alright cool, see you later!" She left the room.

"Hey, welcome back girlie", said Ms. Lucy, the staff member from the year prior as she peeked her head in and smiled. "The shower is all yours today. Go ahead and get that done and I'll let you know what we got going for you today, k? Here's a towel and some clean clothes." From that, I knew they had already briefed about me. I was already sure I would be on red, lockdown, for a while. I did as she said and once done, I sat down on my bed to give myself a moment to take it all in, as to what was happening. A few minutes into sitting there, I had a nice surprise.

"Well hey there. I'm glad to see you're still here." Kelsey said jokingly. Making her way into the room. She sat next to me on my bed.

"Very funny." I rolled my eyes.

"I kid. How are you feeling today?" She asked me with concern.

"Alright, I guess. Just excited to know how to begin the process of emancipation." I said with a question.

"Well easy there girlfriend, you just got here. Don't you wanna know about the benefits of staying in care until you're eighteen?" she replied.

"Like what?" I asked.

"Well, for starters, you would have a full ride to any school in Texas. Tuition, living assistants and all." She smiled.

"Eh. I'm not sure if I even wanna go to college. I still have to catch up in high school. If I do decide to go, I'll figure out a way to make it happen." I said confidently.

"Well you just have life all figured out then don't you?" Kelsey said with sarcasm.

"I don't know… maybe? All I know is I don't wanna be in foster care anymore. That's that whole reason I turned myself in. To be able to get back in school, catch up and be emancipated. I can live on my own if I'm legal, Kelsey. I know I can. I can get a job and pay my bills." I said with all the confidence I could muster. "And go to school?" She asked with doubt.

"Yes. I know I can." I replied quickly.

"Well okay. I believe you. First, just hang tight around here for a little while and we'll see what we can get figured out okay?" Kelsey said.

"How long is a little while?" I asked with impatience building up already.

"I don't know, three months maybe?" she said, thinking.

"Three months! That's forever!" I exclaimed.

"Girl. You were gone for nearly a year. Did it seem that long?" She fired back at me.

"Well… kind of." I admitted.

"Okay well, three months isn't that long. Let these people do their job in helping you into an academy to catch up on your schooling. Word is, if you work hard at it, you can catch up with the class you were in before you left for the next school year. It'll be like you never missed a beat." That really brought hope to my soul. The last thing I wanted was to be behind yet another grade. And I desperately wanted to graduate with my friends back in Brownfield.

"So, I have one thing that you left here last year that I can't give to anyone else because it has your name on it." Kelsey's tone softened a little more.

"Yeah? What's that?" I asked curiously. She reached inside of her oversized brown purse and pulled out my bible. My pink, teal, and brown Bible with my name, Brandy Tijerina beautifully engraved on the bottom right corner. My foster parents, Tod and Kimberly had given it to me as a Christmas gift a few years back. She handed it to me. I looked at it remembering the time I unwrapped it and became disappointed that it was a Bible. *What the heck am I gonna do with this? I wanted the new Mariah Carey CD, and they got me a Bible?* I remembered thinking. From then it sat on my room TV collecting dust.

"Thank you." I looked up at her with eyes of gratitude. Remembering what had happened just the night before.

"So, does that mean you want it?" She asked.

"Yeah, I'll hold onto it." I replied honestly and friend, let me tell you. I did much more than just hold onto it. When Kelsey left that day, I opened that book somewhat out of boredom. To this day, it sits on my bookshelf completely worn. If I pick it up, it almost falls apart if I'm not careful. That Bible holds a special place in my heart. It showed me how truly alive and powerful God's word is. When it says that it's sharper than any double-edged sword (Hebrews 4:12), it means just that. His word spiritually penetrated my heart, and my heart has never been the same once receiving its truth. Oh how surreal the encounter truly is once we surrender to the God of all creation and receive His Holy Spirit. And the profoundness in how He speaks to us through that. And how every answer to every problem truly lays on those thin pages with power waiting to be read and applied to our lives.

After three months of staying at the children's home, I was released and became emancipated. And with God's help and guidance, I was able to confidently catch up in school, work two jobs, have my own home, pay my bills, plus finish high school and walk the stage to receive my high school diploma with my class. All God. I truly could not have done it without the strength and help He gave me.

That chapter of my life ended and began in April of 2009. Today I write this God story in the year of 2020. Meaning I have been following Jesus for eleven years as of now. Let me tell you, it has been one heck of a crazy beautiful journey. Jesus Christ has walked with me, taught me how to forgive the family friend that raped me. Even gave me the courage to walk up to him to tell him I forgive him and then pray for him. Turns out, what he did to me had been eating him alive for all of those years. God set him free when we prayed. My addiction with marijuana took me a while to fully be set free, I'd fall many times, but He would always help me back up and tell me to try again until I stood strong in that area. His joy was one of the first things He poured into me, demolishing all depression that ever resided in my soul and spirit. He taught me about tithing and being generous and how He'd take care of me financially, always. Four years of walking with Him I was still battling the disease of Bulimia. Until the very last time I had my finger down my throat at age twenty and His still small, yet powerful voice told me "I will teach you to live a healthy life if you give this to me." I surrendered that disease to Him that day and I've passionately loved healthy foods and exercise since. The second year into meeting my husband, He began to teach me about purity. And He wanted me to take it back from the enemy before I got married.

That's a story in itself, however my husband and I did our best to pursue purity before marriage. He and I both are still learning how to have a marriage that God designed in His way. Both coming from family backgrounds where healthy marriages weren't modeled. Fear doesn't even have a chance with me anymore. Sure, it comes knocking every now and then, but since Jesus has taught me how to bind, loose, take authority, and use His word, it never sticks around very long.

Temptations and old ways try to creep every now and then as well, but I now stand as an imperfect yet resilient daughter of the highest God who gives me strength when I am weak. A true lifelong friend of Jesus, a wife to a God-fearing man named Stephen Luna, an ordained minister, a speaker, creator, mentor and now an author. He's opened doors to many jobs where I have had the blessing and honor of helping adults, teens and children to healthy living mentally, spiritually, and physically. All the way to being able to go back to the very place where I surrendered my life to Him and share the gospel with teen girls at The Children's Home of Lubbock. Each place He calls me to, I have a mandate to share what He has done in my life. I have truly found my life purpose and identity. To know Him and make Him known. I am His.

Now again, I want to make it clear that along the way, it hasn't been all rainbows and sunshine. It has all been a continuing process. Peter 1:7 (The Message Translation) states: "Pure gold put in fire comes out of it proved pure; genuine faith put through this suffering comes out proved genuine." So, a bumpy yet peaceful journey sort of speak, but through every valley I ever encounter to this day, and every attack that the enemy tries against me, I know I have a Father holding my hand, walking in the fires with me, and guiding me forward to the mountain tops each year. Strengthening me, encouraging me, sharpening me, and loving me unconditionally; lesson by lesson, faith to faith and glory to glory. Until I see Him face to face.

His power and love that I encountered that year of being seventeen wrecked me for the better. And still does today. He truly showed me how He was with me from the very beginning, sending people to love me in my darkest hours. What it is to have a Father, and how I am never alone. I have always had my Daddy right there with me. It only took a whisper of His name in a children's home room, and He was there to my rescue. My savior. The cross before me, the world behind me, no turning back. Oh, how I look forward to continuing the journey, running my race and fighting the good fight. Never in perfection, but always in process until I see His sweet face, bow at His feet and yell with my entire being "Worthy! Worthy! Worthy!!" Because He is that very thing, WORTHY.

The winds and waves of a horrid hurricane were forced upon me. That hurricane (the enemy) wanted to take me out, break me and uproot me. But little did I know that my roots and the toughness of what I was made out of by a Holy God is what kept me grounded. What the enemy meant for harm, God made it into something so good. Today, only by His grace and goodness, I stand tall like a palm tree. Each time the sun shows its face, my face is up as well, and I've been made able to thrive in it, no matter the amount of heat. (Again, like a palm tree.)

As for my mom and sisters, when my mom was released from prison in 2008, she came out as a completely transformed woman. When I finally got to see and visit her, she was the mom I yearned to have as a little girl. The women she was always meant to be. Godly, sound minded, hardworking, peaceful, joyous and standing firm and tall as well. Set free, completely. She shared with me about her experience in prison. How God had met her in the chapel as she was down on bending knee pleading to give her another chance to be the mother, she knew she could be.

She testifies that she heard the Lord speak "I will give you your children back, my daughter. Seek me every day, and I will be sure to restore your whole life." Sure enough, faithful to His word, just six months after being released, she was granted full and legal custody of my sisters on Christmas Day of 2009. Oh, and just to add a cherry on top, her lawyer didn't charge her a penny. He told her "I just felt the need to truly help you get your girls back." God was truly with my mom.

My sisters are now grown and living their own lives. Both pure at heart and seeking the Lord as well. My mother has been able to raise my only brother, Isaiah, since age 2. (She conceived his sweet self while we were in the system, and when sent to prison he was placed with an aunt until she was released.) He is a young gentleman, with a heart of gold, who I know God has called as well.

Back in 2017, God gave me strength to fully forgive my dad. I searched for him and found him in a prison there in Texas. My husband and I went to visit and from that point forward, he and I have been able to rekindle and are working toward a relationship. Today he is a free, and changed man who stands tall and resilient as well. Again, by the sweet grace and mercy of our Heavenly Father. So, friends, the question I have to leave you with today as we close our time together (for now) is, what struggles are you facing? Generational curses that are circling? What hurts do you have in your heart that beckons for healing? What strongholds and storms are keeping you bent right now? Whether it be anything that I went through, or things that are completely different but still heavy, can I just say (from honest experience) that we have a God who truly desires to help. And not just help, but to take care of you as well. He wants to love you, provide for you, heal you, restore you, set your feet on solid ground and do life with you. Would you believe me if I said that we were created for that? To live a free life in abundance with Jesus Christ daily? That He truly does call you by your name, knows the very number of hairs on your head and hunny, you absolutely do have a divine purpose no matter what anyone else has said, what you have done or where you come from.

If you feel a tug on your heart, why don't you take that step of faith and do what I did when I had no hope for my future in that small room. Cry out to Jesus from the depth of your heart. Humble yourself, ask Him to forgive you and to place His spirit within you. Let Him know that you believe that He sent His only Son to die for your sins. And with your hands up in surrender, let Him begin a good work in you. I can promise you when I say He will respond, and it will be the best decision you could ever make in your entire life. It's not too late, you're not too far gone, and you're not too young and you're not too old. Because if He could save wretch like me, my mom and my dad, then Beloved, He will gladly and is excitedly waiting to do it for you too. You too can be like a palm tree. Where you'll stand with witnesses and be able to say "I bent, but I didn't break. I now stand tall and resilient by His spirit."

If you are saying "girl, I know exactly what you mean. I've been walking this faith walk for some time too." Well praise God! Seriously, praise Him! We are in this and we are better together! I am cheering you on as I write this. Keep running your race! Share your story of what God has done in your life, and the good news! You never know who's watching you as an example, and who will be inspired by your unique voice.

Glory to the highest, forever and ever! Amen.

"The righteous shall flourish like a palm tree, He shall grow like a cedar in Lebanon. Those who are planted in the house of the Lord shall flourish in the courts of our

God. They shall still bear fruit in old age; They shall be fresh and flourishing, to declare that the Lord is upright; He is my rock and there is no unrighteousness in Him." Psalms 92:12-15 (New King James Version)

Many blessings my sweet friend. With so much love,

- Brandy Luna

Made in the USA
Las Vegas, NV
11 March 2021